NEW FRONTIERS FOR ENTERTAINMENT COMPUTING

IFIP – The International Federation for Information Processing

IFIP was founded in 1960 under the auspices of UNESCO, following the First World Computer Congress held in Paris the previous year. An umbrella organization for societies working in information processing, IFIP's aim is two-fold: to support information processing within its member countries and to encourage technology transfer to developing nations. As its mission statement clearly states,

> IFIP's mission is to be the leading, truly international, apolitical organization which encourages and assists in the development, exploitation and application of information technology for the benefit of all people.

IFIP is a non-profitmaking organization, run almost solely by 2500 volunteers. It operates through a number of technical committees, which organize events and publications. IFIP's events range from an international congress to local seminars, but the most important are:

• The IFIP World Computer Congress, held every second year;
• Open conferences;
• Working conferences.

The flagship event is the IFIP World Computer Congress, at which both invited and contributed papers are presented. Contributed papers are rigorously refereed and the rejection rate is high.

As with the Congress, participation in the open conferences is open to all and papers may be invited or submitted. Again, submitted papers are stringently refereed.

The working conferences are structured differently. They are usually run by a working group and attendance is small and by invitation only. Their purpose is to create an atmosphere conducive to innovation and development. Refereeing is less rigorous and papers are subjected to extensive group discussion.

Publications arising from IFIP events vary. The papers presented at the IFIP World Computer Congress and at open conferences are published as conference proceedings, while the results of the working conferences are often published as collections of selected and edited papers.

Any national society whose primary activity is in information may apply to become a full member of IFIP, although full membership is restricted to one society per country. Full members are entitled to vote at the annual General Assembly, National societies preferring a less committed involvement may apply for associate or corresponding membership. Associate members enjoy the same benefits as full members, but without voting rights. Corresponding members are not represented in IFIP bodies. Affiliated membership is open to non-national societies, and individual and honorary membership schemes are also offered.

NEW FRONTIERS FOR ENTERTAINMENT COMPUTING

IFIP 20th World Computer Congress, First IFIP Entertainment Computing Symposium (ECS 2008), September 7-10, 2008, Milano, Italy

Edited by

Paolo Ciancarini
University of Bologna
Italy

Ryohei Nakatsu
Kwansai Gakuin University
Japan

Matthias Rauterberg
Eindhoven University of Technology
The Netherlands

Marco Roccetti
University of Bologna
Italy

 Springer

Editors

Paolo Ciancarini
University of Bologna
Italy

Ryohei Nakatsu
Kwansai Gakuin University
Japan

Matthias Rauterberg
Eindhoven University of Technology
The Netherlands

Marco Roccetti
University of Bologna
Italy

p. cm. (IFIP International Federation for Information Processing, a Springer Series in Computer Science)

ISSN: 1571-5736 / 1861-2288 (Internet)
ISBN: 978-1-4419-3521-2   e-ISBN: 978-0-387-09701-5

Printed on acid-free paper

springer.com

IFIP 2008 World Computer Congress (WCC'08)

Message from the Chairs

Every two years, the International Federation for Information Processing hosts a major event which showcases the scientific endeavours of its over one hundred Technical Committees and Working Groups. 2008 sees the 20th World Computer Congress (WCC 2008) take place for the first time in Italy, in Milan from 7-10 September 2008, at the MIC - Milano Convention Centre. The Congress is hosted by the Italian Computer Society, AICA, under the chairmanship of Giulio Occhini.

The Congress runs as a federation of co-located conferences offered by the different IFIP bodies, under the chairmanship of the scientific chair, Judith Bishop. For this Congress, we have a larger than usual number of thirteen conferences, ranging from Theoretical Computer Science, to Open Source Systems, to Entertainment Computing. Some of these are established conferences that run each year and some represent new, breaking areas of computing. Each conference had a call for papers, an International Programme Committee of experts and a thorough peer reviewed process. The Congress received 661 papers for the thirteen conferences, and selected 375 from those representing an acceptance rate of 56% (averaged over all conferences).

An innovative feature of WCC 2008 is the setting aside of two hours each day for cross-sessions relating to the integration of business and research, featuring the use of IT in Italian industry, sport, fashion and so on. This part is organized by Ivo De Lotto. The Congress will be opened by representatives from government bodies and Societies associated with IT in Italy.

This volume is one of fourteen volumes associated with the scientific conferences and the industry sessions. Each covers a specific topic and separately or together they form a valuable record of the state of computing research in the world in 2008. Each volume was prepared for publication in the Springer IFIP Series by the conference's volume editors. The overall Chair for all the volumes published for the Congress is John Impagliazzo.

For full details on the Congress, refer to the webpage http://www.wcc2008.org.

Judith Bishop, South Africa, Co-Chair, International Program Committee
Ivo De Lotto, Italy, Co-Chair, International Program Committee
Giulio Occhini, Italy, Chair, Organizing Committee
John Impagliazzo, United States, Publications Chair

WCC 2008 Scientific Conferences

TC12	AI	Artificial Intelligence 2008
TC10	BICC	Biologically Inspired Cooperative Computing
WG 5.4	CAI	Computer-Aided Innovation (Topical Session)
WG 10.2	DIPES	Distributed and Parallel Embedded Systems
TC14	ECS	Entertainment Computing Symposium
TC3	ED_L2L	Learning to Live in the Knowledge Society
WG 9.7 TC3	HCE3	History of Computing and Education 3
TC13	HCI	Human Computer Interaction
TC8	ISREP	Information Systems Research, Education and Practice
WG 12.6	KMIA	Knowledge Management in Action
TC2 WG 2.13	OSS	Open Source Systems
TC11	IFIP SEC	Information Security Conference
TC1	TCS	Theoretical Computer Science

IFIP
- is the leading multinational, apolitical organization in Information and Communications Technologies and Sciences
- is recognized by United Nations and other world bodies
- represents IT Societies from 56 countries or regions, covering all 5 continents with a total membership of over half a million
- links more than 3500 scientists from Academia and Industry, organized in more than 101 Working Groups reporting to 13 Technical Committees
- sponsors 100 conferences yearly providing unparalleled coverage from theoretical informatics to the relationship between informatics and society including hardware and software technologies, and networked information systems

Details of the IFIP Technical Committees and Working Groups can be found on the website at http://www.ifip.org.

Preface

Welcome to the International 1st IFIP Entertainment Computing Symposium on "New Frontiers for Entertainment Computing" (ECS-2008), which is part of the 20th IFIP World Computer Congress, to be held in Milano, Italy, September 7-10, 2008. On behalf of all the people who made this conference happen, we wish to welcome you to this international event.

During the past years the IFIP World Computer Congress offered an opportunity for researchers and practitioners to present their findings and research results in several prominent areas of computer science and engineering. This year, among other activities, IFIP launches a new initiative focused on all the relevant issues concerning Computing and Entertainment. As a result, the 2-day technical program of the Entertainment Computing Symposium (ECS) will provide a forum to address, explore and exchange information on the state-of-the-art of computer based entertainment and allied technologies, their design and use, and their impact on the society.

Within the emerging field of entertainment technologies, we need to tackle a broad range of technology, management and design issues, and we need to become familiar with newly introduced techniques and current applications. To this aim, the spectrum of papers presented at ECS will cover topics from system modeling and simulation to physics, professional gaming products, multimedia visualization, artificial intelligence, robotics, plus others designed to provide a wide range of topics as reflected in the technical program of the Conference. Those contributed papers have undergone a detailed peer paper review and helped us to achieve this goal. Special recognition goes to each of the contributing authors for their dedication and effort in their field of research. Our technical program bears testimony to the many challenges that the field of entertainment computing is stimulating. In particular the ECS technical program include the following papers:

Enhancing Artificial Intelligence in Games by Learning the Opponent's Playing Style
Fabio Aiolli and Claudio Palazzi

Using Game Engines for Visualization in Scientific Applications
Karl-Ingo Friese, Marc Herrlich and Franz-Erich Wolter

An Interactive Visual Canon Platform
Mathias Funk and Christoph Bartneck

Physical Emotion Induction and Its Use in Entertainment: Lessons Learned
Ralph Kok and Joost Broekens

Networked Virtual Marionette Theater
Daisuke Ninomiya, Kohji Miyazaki and Ryohei Nakatsu

Entertainment Computing in the Orbit
Matthias Rauterberg, Mark Neerincx, Karl Tuyls and Jack van Loon

A Collaborative Science Learning Game Environment for Informal Science Education: DinoQuest Online
Walt Scacchi and Robert Nideffer

Construction and Evaluation of a Robot Dance System
Kuniya Shinozaki, Akitsugu Iwatani and Ryohei Nakatsu

Context-aware fun and games with Bluetooth
Andy Sloane and Chris Dennett

Automatic Comic Generation from Game Log
Ruck Thawonmas and Tomonori Shuda

i.plot
Naoko Tosa and Seigow Matsuoka

Analysis and Generation of Japanese Folktales Based on Vladimir Propp's Methodology
Takenori Wama and Ryohei Nakatsu.

In addition to all the accepted papers, we assembled a program comprising also two keynote speeches given by Dr. Jason Chown (Sony Computer Entertainment Europe) and by Dr. Nicolas Gaume (Mimesis Republic, France).

On behalf of the Organizing Committee, we would like to extend our personal thanks to all the members of the International Program Committee, namely to: Christoph Bartneck, NL; Brad Bushman, US; Marc Cavazza, UK; Adrian Cheok, SG; Konstantinos Chorianopoulos, DE; Sidney Fels, CA; Nahum Gershon, US, Jan Klabbers, NL, David Obrazalek, CZ, Zhigeng Pan, CN, Claudio Pinhanez, US, Andy Sloane, UK, Bill Swartout, US, Naoko Tosa, JP, Gino Yu, HK.

Our sincere gratitude goes to them for their hard work in reviewing and selecting the best papers to be presented from all the received submissions. The success of this conference is credited to them, as well as to session chairs, presenters and attendees. We are indebted also to the many individuals who have helped us to make ECS a successful event. A special thank goes to Gian Piero Favini, who took care of the conference management site and prepared the draft of the camera ready of these proceedings.

Paolo Ciancarini
Symposium Chair and Editor
University of Bologna, Italy

Ryohei Nakatsu
Symposium Chair and Editor
Interactive & Digital Media Institute, Singapore

Matthias Rauterberg
Program Chair and Editor
Eindhoven University of Technology, The Netherlands

Marco Roccetti
Symposium Chair and Editor
University of Bologna, Italy

Contents

Contents

Enhancing Artificial Intelligence in Games by Learning the Opponent's Playing Style

Fabio Aiolli and Claudio Enrico Palazzi

Abstract As virtual environments are becoming graphically nearly realistic, the need for a satisfying Artificial Intelligence (AI) is perceived as more and more important by game players. In particular, what players have to face nowadays in terms of AI is not far from what was available at the beginning of the video games era. Even nowadays, the AI of almost all games is based on a finite set of actions/reactions whose sequence can be easily predicted by expert players. As a result, the game soon becomes too obvious to still be fun. Instead, machine learning techniques could be employed to classify a player's behavior and consequently adapt the game's AI; the competition against the AI would become more stimulant and the fun of the game would last longer. To this aim, we consider a game where both the player and the AI have a limited information about the current game state and where it is part of the game to guess the information hidden by the opponent. We demonstrate how machine learning techniques could be easily implemented in this context to improve the AI by making it adaptive with respect to the strategy of a specific player.

1 Introduction

Games embody one of the main revenue sources for the digital entertainment industry, attracting every day a multitude of new customers and astonishing them with tremendous advancements in terms of graphics quality. Indeed, the current 3D graphics is far away from the flashing pixels of the first video games. Unfortunately,

Fabio Aiolli
Pure and Applied Math Department, University of Padova, Via Trieste 63 - 35131, Padova, Italy, e-mail: aiolli@math.unipd.it

Claudio Enrico Palazzi
Pure and Applied Math Department, University of Padova, Via Trieste 63 - 35131, Padova, Italy, e-mail: cpalazzi@math.unipd.it

Please use the following format when citing this chapter:

Aiolli, F. and Palazzi, C.E., 2008, in IFIP International Federation for Information Processing, Volume 279; *New Frontiers for Entertainment Computing*; Paolo Ciancarini, Ryohei Nakatsu, Matthias Rauterberg, Marco Roccetti; (Boston: Springer), pp. 1–10.

the same level of advancement did not happen in another very important aspect of gaming: the Artificial Intelligence (AI) that commands the virtual opponent of a player. Current games still rely on decision trees with almost deterministic sequences of actions and reactions. Standard difficulty degrees are generally offered to provide players with harder virtual opponents. Yet, these degrees are generally associated with just i) deeper levels that the AI can access in the decision tree rather than adapting its decisions to the human opponent, or ii) an improvement of the quality of the virtual opponent's features (e.g., speed, armor, weapons) rather than improving its ability in using them. Expert players can hence quickly find weak spots in the AI, adopting a routine of actions that (almost) always leads to victory; at the same time, the game quickly gets boring.

Viceversa, part of the fun in playing against another human opponent relies on the fact that she/he can uncover possible winning tactics and adapt to them, thus prolonging the challenge and the fun considerably. Providing this adaptation ability also to the AI is going to become a crucial feature of future game releases, determining their market success. Since its importance, we show how adaptation in game's intelligence can be generated through machine learning techniques that model a human's behavior.

Furthermore, classic searching techniques may not be feasible for certain games. Indeed, games can be classified into two main categories depending on whether participants have or not a complete knowledge of the game state at any moment. Typical exemplars of the two classes are represented by Chess and Poker, respectively. When players have just a limited knowledge of the game state, resorting to traditional search in decision trees may result in an AI as effective as a random decision maker. Instead, machine learning techniques could be exploited to mimic the humans's ability in intuiting the opponent's intentions after several game sessions.

As a case study for this subject, we consider *Ghosts*[1], a simple board game played by two opponents and that had not yet a computer based version. The game is particularly interesting for our study as players do not have a complete knowledge of the game state: they can both see the position of game pieces on the board, but they cannot see the type of the opponent's ones. Depending on this information, different tactics would be adopted (i.e., attack the opponent's piece, leave it alone, run away from it). Therefore, in order to win, a player has also to infer the type of each of the opponent's pieces. This information can be extracted from the player's behavior, also keeping in mind that different players can adopt different strategies, for instance, by resorting more or less frequently to bluffing.

In this work we stepped through different phases. First, we have generated a computer based version of *Ghosts* that can be played both against an AI and against another human opponent. Second, we have collected and analyzed tens of game sessions to extract behavior features. Third, we have endowed the AI with machine learning capabilities so as to associate the behavior features of a specific player with a presumed type of a piece. In essence, by observing how a player acts in different

---

[1] The board game has been invented by Alex Randolph and is sold in Germany by *Drei Magier Spiele*. Its original (German) name is: *Die guten und die bösen Geister*, i.e., good and bad ghosts; for brevity, we simply name it *Ghosts*.

game state configurations, the AI becomes able to classify tactics employed by that specific player and to adapt to them. Finally, we have tested the system, proving its ability in profiling the player's strategy and adapting to it.

The rest of the paper is organized as follows. In Section 2 we review some background in game-related machine learning and describe the specific game we have considered as a case study. The machine learning capabilities we devised to improve the game AI is presented in Section 3. Section 4 describes the experimental scenario and reports the corresponding outcomes. Finally, in Section 5 conclusions and future directions for this research work are provided.

2 Background

Delving into the Internet, the first video game seems to be a simple tennis-for-two created by Higginbotham in 1958 to entertain visitors of the Brookhaven National Laboratory, a US nuclear research lab in Upton, New York. Only one year later, Samuel proposed the first self-learning gaming program, i.e., Checkers, that represented a very early demonstration of the fundamental concept of AI in games [12]. Nowadays, all video games include some AI that may act as a virtual opponent or as a component of the game itself. Yet, the AI of current games show only little advancements if compared to its ancestors; only for few specific games the AI has achieved great improvements (e.g., Chess [6]).

In general, games can be categorized into two main classes: games where the players possess perfect information about the current game state (e.g., Chess, Tic-tac-toe) and games where players can rely only on imperfect information (e.g., Poker, Rock-paper-scissors). In the former case, all the information related to a certain game state are known by players; whereas in the latter, players may not be aware of some information such as the opponent's cards or the placement of the opponent's pieces on the board.

The AI of *perfect information games* can easily evaluate a given game state by just searching all possible continuations to a fixed depth. For this kind of games, the main problem in developing an AI is related to the capability of pre-computing correct evaluations of each game state and then storing and retrieving them in an efficient manner [1, 9, 5].

Instead, with *imperfect information games*, deep search may not be feasible and storing pre-computed evaluations may not result in significant improvements in the playing strength [3, 8]. In these case, techniques like temporal difference learning are also unsuitable as the intermediate states of a game are only partially determined [11]. Alternative solutions have hence to be explored to enhance the level of the AI. For instance, *simulation search* [13, 2, 10, 14] evaluates the possible next moves by self-playing a multitude of simulated game sessions, considering the current state as the starting point and utilizing different values for the indeterministic parameters (i.e., dice rolls, cards held by the opponent player, etc.). To generate real-time responses during the game, these simulations can be run before the game and statistics can be stored to be promptly available during the game. Unfortunately, the branching factor of certain games may considerably limit the effectiveness of this technique.

Instead, we propose a new machine learning approach that mimics the human's ability in evaluating important information about the current game state that goes beyond, for instance, the board position. In essence, our mechanism models the opponent's behavior over several game sessions so as to be able to exploit the weaknesses and the repetitive behaviors of the considered human player.

2.1 A Representative Case Study: Ghosts

For our experiments, we need a simple, yet representative exemplar of imperfect information game. *Ghosts* embodies a perfect case as, not only it belongs to this class of games, but it is also governed by few simple rules, which follow. Two players have to place 8 ghosts each at the back of a 6x6 board as shown in Fig. 1. Each player has 4 good ghosts and 4 bad ghosts, but the information about which are good and which bad is hidden to the opponent player. Each turn a player moves one of her/his ghosts one square vertically or horizontally; if by doing so the ghost is moved onto an opponent's ghost, the latter is captured by the former. In order to win, different possibilities are available to a player: i) having all of her/his bad ghosts captured by the opponent player, ii) capturing all the good ghosts of the opponent player, iii) moving one of her/his good ghosts off the board from one of the opponent's corner squares. Clearly, one of the interesting aspects of *Ghosts* is its bluffing element which is differently utilized by different human players.

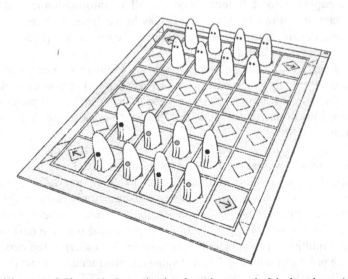

Fig. 1 Initial set-up of *Ghosts* (the image is taken from the manual of the board game).

3 Enhancing the AI with Player Profiling Capabilities

The most interesting problems in game AI are typically grouped with respect to certain characteristics. One of the most intriguing characteristics is how much information is available to the players. This leads us to distinguish between perfect information games and imperfect information games as discussed in Section 2. Clearly, the latter is more interesting as it represents a more challenging case.

Ghosts embodies a good case study as it falls in the imperfect information games class, yet, it simple enough to be analyzed. In *Ghosts* a player does not have any information about the type of the opponent's ghosts (i.e., good or bad); thereby, any search state space based technique, e.g. min-max algorithms, will fail miserably. In other words, without any other heuristic judgement, the behavior of a machine driven player could not be better than a any trivial random player.

Indeed, in order to plan its moves, an AI algorithm would certainly benefit from some other source of information about the type of the opponent's ghosts (the missing information). In this work, we propose to get this additional information from the playing style of a player. The basic assumption we make is that different players have different playing behaviors (being aggressive, bluffing, etc.) and they tend to move pieces of a certain type in a similar way when facing similar game situations. Specifically, our claim is that knowing the playing style of a player, it is possible to recognize the type of a given ghost by its moves. We can then use a machine learning algorithm [11] to compile a behavior profile of good and bad pieces of a player. During future game sessions, this knowledge can be used to predict the type of a ghost in the board and possibly to define higher level game heuristics, like min-max algorithms, based on this predictions.

The machine learning methodology we have used is very simple and it is based on a prototype-based algorithm. Specifically, for each player, a prototype of good and bad ghosts is trained based on 17 features which have been considered informative to determine the nature of a ghost in the game.

In particular, the following features have been chosen: 8 features with binary values representing which was the initial position of the piece on the board among the eight possible ones, 5 features representing the moves of the piece during the game session (if it is the first piece that the player moved, if it is the second piece that the player moved, the number of backward, forward, and lateral moves already performed by that piece), and the remaining 4 features representing the piece's behavior when it has been under threat of being captured (how many times it has reacted by capturing the opponent piece, how many times it has escaped by moving to another board position, how many times it has remained on its position, and how many times it has moved from its square to threat another opponent's piece).

To build the prototype for a player, our algorithm needs first to collect data, i.e., the training set, from previous game sessions with the same player. For each of these sessions and for each piece a corresponding feature vector is built according to the criteria above which are based on the behavior of the piece in the game. The prototype for good (or bad) pieces is then determined as the average among the feature vectors representing good (or bad) pieces. More formally, given $G = \{g_1, \ldots, g_n\}$

the set of feature vectors for good pieces of a given player, and $B = \{b_1, \ldots, b_n\}$ the set of available feature vectors for bad pieces of the same player, the prototype vectors are computed in the following way:

$$P_G = \frac{1}{n} \sum_{i=1}^{n} g_i, \text{ and } P_B = \frac{1}{n} \sum_{i=1}^{n} b_i. \tag{1}$$

Now, let be given a new feature vector f representing the profile of a piece of unknown type on the board; a badness score can hence be computed by using the normalized distance with respect to the player prototypes, i.e.,

$$s(f) = \frac{d(f, P_G) - d(f, P_B)}{d(f, P_G) + d(f, P_B)} \tag{2}$$

where $d(x, y)$ is the Euclidean distance between vectors x and y. Note that, the score is always a number between -1 (definitely good) and $+1$ (definitely bad).

On each move in the middle of a game session, the prediction of the type of the pieces on the board is performed in the following way. First, since the exact number of good and bad pieces (n_g and n_b, respectively) still on the board is a known information, a badness score for each of these pieces can be computed by utilizing (2). Then, the pieces are ranked based on this score and the n_b highest score pieces are predicted to be bad pieces.

The error committed in a prediction is computed as the number of bad pieces which are actually predicted as good ones. Needless to say, with the ranking method we used to discriminate between bad and good pieces, this error also corresponds to the number of good pieces which are incorrectly predicted as bad.

4 Experimental Results

In this section, we report on experimental results that show the effectiveness of our profiling procedure. To train our machine learning algorithm, we have generated a computer based version of *Ghosts* and collected a set of 81 game session logs for a player who was playing against other human players.

4.1 Profiling Evaluation in a Single Game Session

In this first set of experiments, we aim at studying how the prediction error decreases in a game as ghosts' profiles become more and more informative. This prediction improvement is naturally caused by the fact that some of the features for a piece can be still unavailable or underestimated at the very beginning of a game session, thus generating a bad estimate of the pieces' profiles. Yet, the precision of the predictor quickly improves as the game session continues. This represents a desirable property as, in general, it is not so important to have a very low error when the game is at the very beginning, whereas it becomes crucial as the game session proceeds.

In particular, Fig. 2 plots the percentage of error that the machine learning algorithm performs during a single game. The same game experiment has been repeated five times (labeled in the chart as *g1*, *g2*, *g3*, *g4*, and *g5*, respectively): 50% of error means that two good (and two bad) ghosts over 4 were wrongly labeled as bad (good), 25% represents the case with only one good (and one bad) ghost wrongly labeled, and 0% is the when the system is providing perfect type prediction for all the ghosts. As expected, the error drops as the number of moves increases.

4.2 Profiling Evaluation with Varying Training Set Size

In a second set of experiments, the performance of the algorithm has been tested considering several game sessions against the same human player. To this aim, an estimate of the mean error in each game has been computed by using a leave-one-out procedure. This measure, very common in the machine learning community, was used as it provably gives a very good estimate of the error a learning algorithm will make on future games on average. Specifically, for each available game session

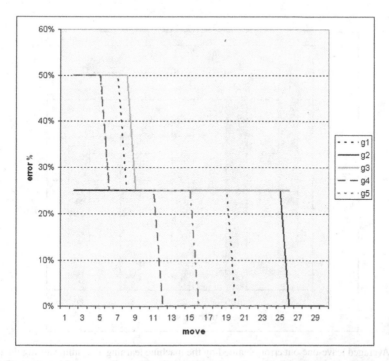

Fig. 2 Percentage of error performed by the machine learning algorithm when playing 5 games.

log, the mean error (the number of mistakes out of the number of guesses) has been computed using the model obtained by training on the remaining 80 game logs. All these results have been averaged to obtain a final estimation of the algorithm's performance. The leave-one-out estimation result has been 26.3% error.

Aimed at showing how the performance of the algorithm improves when employing higher numbers of training game logs, we have exploited the leave-one-out procedure also considering different training set sizes (i.e., 5, 10, 25, 50, 80). For each chosen size of the training log set, we have repeated the procedure each time considering a different left-out log; the averaged resulting error percentages are reported in Fig. 3.

As expected, with larger sizes of the training set, the machine learning algorithm is able to build more reliable profiles of the players, improving the performance of the prediction system. In particular, the error drops from 42%, when only 5 training logs are used, to 26.3% with 80 training logs.

5 Conclusion

AI is becoming a crucial, albeit still neglected aspect in games. Imperfect information games are particularly affected by the lack of smart virtual opponents thus

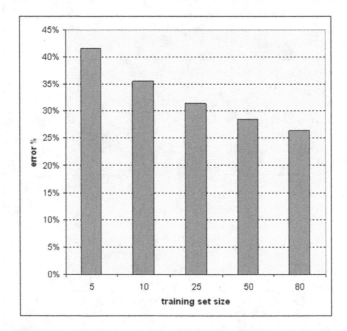

Fig. 3 Averaged leave-one-out error obtained by the machine learning algorithm varying the number of game logs used for training.

demanding new technical solutions. To this aim, we have designed and tested a new approach that improves the capability of the machine player by allowing it to adapt to its human opponent and exploit her/his weaknesses. In particular, through repeated game sessions, the AI models the behavior of a human player so as to be able to employ the strategy that best fits that player. Moreover, this profiling method can be easily plugged into any standard AI or temporal difference learning based algorithm to enhance their performance.

In order to test our solution, we have deployed a computer based version of *Ghost*, a simple, yet general, two-player imperfect information game. Results gathered during our experimental evaluation demonstrates how our approach may allow the AI to adapt to the player.

Our experiments have to be intended as proof of concept for the benefits that player profiling can produce when considering imperfect information games. We have hence used a very simple machine learning algorithm to test the viability of the general method. This work can hence be extended in several research directions. For instance, we intend to improve the methodology by using state-of-the-art machine learning algorithms such as, for instance, Support Vector Machines [15], and to enhance the set of features used to profile the opponent's behavior. Moreover, we also plan to apply our solution to more complex imperfect information games such as *Invisible Chess* and *Kriegspiel* which are heterodox Chess variation in which players are not informed of their opponents position and moves [4, 7].

Acknowledgement

Our deep gratitude goes to Ivan Mazzarelli and Federico Giardina for their technical contribution in developing the computer based version of the game and the experimental set-up.

References

1. Allis, V. (1988). A knowledge-based approach of Connect-Four the game is solved: White wins. Masters Thesis, Department of Mathematics and Computer Science, Vrije Universiteit, Amsterdam, Netherlands.
2. Billings, D., Pena L., Schaeffer, J., Szafron, D. (1999). Using probabilistic knowledge and simulation to play Poker. In Proceedings of the 16th National Conference on Artificial Intelligence (AAAI-99), Orlando, Florida, 697-703.
3. Billings, D. (2000). The first international RoShamBo programming competition. International Computer Games Association Journal 23(1), 42-50.
4. Bud, A., Albrecht, D., Nicholson, A., Zukerman, I. (2001). Playing Invisible Chess with Information-Theoretic Advisors. In Proc. 2001 AAAI Spring Symposium on Game Theoretic and Decision Theoretic Agents, California, USA, 6-15.
5. Buro, M. (1997). The Othello match of the year: Takeshi Murakami vs. Logistello. International Computer Chess Association Journal 20(3), 189-193.

6. Campbell, M. S. (1999). Knowledge discovery in Deep Blue. Communications of the ACM, 42(11), 65-67.
7. Ciancarini, P., Dalla Libera, F., Maran, F. (1997). Decision Making under Uncertainty: A Rational Approach to Kriegspiel. In J. van den Herik and J. Uiterwijk, editors, Advances in Computer Chess 8, 277-298.
8. Egnor, D. (2000). Iocaine powder. International Computer Games Association Journal 23(1), 33-35.
9. Gasser, R. (1995). Efficiently harnessing computational resources for exhaustive search. Ph. D. thesis, ETH, Zurich, Switzerland.
10. Ginsberg, M. L. (1999). GIB: Steps toward an expert-level Bridge-playing program. In Proceedings of the International Joint Conference on Artificial Intelligence (IJCAI-99), Stockholm, Sweden, 584-589.
11. Mitchell T. (1997). *Machine learning*. McGraw Hill.
12. Samuel, A. L. (1959). Some studies in machine learning using the game of Checkers. IBM Journal of Research and Development 3(3), 211-229.
13. Schaeffer, J. (2000). The games computers (and people) play. InM. V. Zelkowitz (Ed.), Advances in Computers, 50, 189-266.
14. Sheppard B. (1999). Mastering Scrabble. IEEE Intelligent Systems 14(6), 15-16.
15. Vapnik V. (1995). *The nature of statistical learning theory*. Springer-Verlag.

Using Game Engines for Visualization in Scientific Applications

Karl-Ingo Friese, Marc Herrlich, and Franz-Erich Wolter

Abstract In recent years, the computer gaming industry has become a large and important market and impressive amounts of money are spent on the development of new game engines. In contrast to their development costs, the price for the final product is very low compared to a professional 3D visualization/animation program. The idea to use this potential for other purposes than gaming seems obvious. This work gives a review on three *Serious Gaming* projects, analyzes the encountered problems in a greater context and reflects the pros and cons of using game engines for scientific applications in general.

1 Introduction

In 2002 the University of Hannover held its yearly open house day and our department had a small presentation as well. One of the projects we showed was a diploma thesis, showing caves, i.e. former mines, reconstructed from laser scan data. The focus of the thesis was the reconstruction itself, not the visualization, aiming for engineering post processing. Still, it was possible to show the reconstructed cave walls in some way (figure 1).

At that open day we had a visitor who was an archaeologist. She was very interested in the caves, since they had just discovered a new cave with bones and wall paintings in a nearby mountain area, which was inaccessible for a larger public. When we told her that our programs could show only the *outside* of a cave, without the possibility to *walk through it* she was a bit disappointed.

Karl-Ingo Friese, e-mail: kif@gdv.uni-hannover.de
Franz-Erich Wolter, e-mail: few@gdv.uni-hannover.de
Institute of Man-Machine-Communication, Leibniz Universität Hannover, Germany

Marc Herrlich, e-mail: mh@tzi.de
Research Group Digital Media, Universität Bremen, Germany

Please use the following format when citing this chapter:

Friese, K-I., Herrlich, M. and Wolter, F-E., 2008, in IFIP International Federation for Information Processing, Volume 279; *New Frontiers for Entertainment Computing*; Paolo Ciancarini, Ryohei Nakatsu, Matthias Rauterberg, Marco Roccetti; (Boston: Springer), pp. 11–22.

The idea to visualize these caves also from the *inside* was born. The goal was to write a small application that would allow a more natural form of showing our caves. What we wanted was an application, which would allow to run in a first-person-perspective through a cave-like virtual dungeon and it was obvious that such applications already existed in the form of computer games or to be more precise: first-person-shooters.

Compared to professional scientific visualization software, computer games have to favor real-time rendering over physical correctness and data accuracy. We took the challenge to see if we could visualize our reconstructed cave with a 3D computer game, which, after solving some problems at the beginning, turned out to be possible.

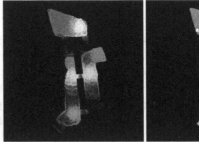

Fig. 1 A (reconstructed) cave with three chambers, seen from the outside. The different colors represent the different laser measurements.

Since then, several projects using computer games to visualize scientific data followed. This paper gives an overview of three of them, classify them in the context of *Serious Gaming* and finally reflect if and when the use of game engines in scientific applications can be useful.

2 What has been done?

The terms *Serious Games* and *Serious Gaming* are used in the literature to describe very different application scenarios. While the concept of *Serious Games* is originally stemming from the area of game-based learning and education [1, 17], today it is more generally used to describe a whole spectrum of applications [14]. In this sense, the area of *Serious Games* incorporates all aspects of applying computer game technology to non-entertainment uses, including but not limited to simulation, visualization and VR. For this paper we are only considering 3D-games, not puzzles, 2D-shooters, etc. and will use the following definition of *Serious Games*:

Definition 1. Every application that makes significant use of game technology and is not primarily intended for pure entertainment is a *Serious Game*.

Historically, games were designed and implemented on a case-to-case basis, leaving only little room for easy modification and reuse. Therefore, the usefulness of game technology for other application areas was somewhat limited. However, this changed with the appearance of the first modern game engines, e.g. the Quake or Unreal series, which provided better modularity. Today, developers can choose from a number of suitable commercial and non-commercial engines.

In this paper we will focus on the area of visualization using modern computer game engines. Before discussing our own research and results in the following sections, we will present a current overview of the ongoing research and development, focusing on indoor and outdoor GIS and CAD data visualization and interaction.

In 2002, Rhyne [13] argued that scientists today have much to learn from the computer games industry regarding computer graphics, visualization, and interfaces, especially with the background of cluster computing. In this area it is an ongoing trend to build clusters from standard PC hardware instead of specialized workstations or mainframes. In Rhyne's opinion, scientific visualization applications can benefit from computer game technology, as most computer games are optimized for commodity hardware. On the other hand, she states some drawbacks in using computer game engines, especially concerning data accuracy and reliability. She also mentions the traditionally short release cycles in the games industry, which may lead to incomplete or unstable graphics drivers.

While this is certainly true, these short release cycles also have their advantages. Namely the availability and support for new hardware and software features. Furthermore, as production costs for modern games are exploding, the development processes have matured and there is a specialization taking place that is dividing game companies into technology developers and technology users, which will lead to more robust solutions.

In the same year, Herwig and Paar [10] discussed the suitability of game engines for landscape visualization and planning. They presented different usage scenarios and analyzed the requirements of landscape architects concerning supporting tools and to what extend game engines can solve these problems. They also showed preliminary results of tests conducted with a landscape visualization based on the *Unreal Engine*. Their findings fit in very well with our own research in landscape visualization based on the CryEngine presented in section 3.3.

In the following, we will report on a number of visualization projects, which approximately fall into the same time span as our own projects described thereafter.

In 2001, Freudenberg et al. [6] described a low-cost VR installation powered by the Shark3D game engine. Using commodity hardware, i.e. three standard PCs and beamers, they employed the game engine's built-in rendering and networking features to create a distributed rendering system capable of driving the VR projection in real-time. Their system had enough power reserves to render pre-distorted images to compensate for the spherical projection plane. Opposed to expensive off-the-shelf VR solutions, the game-based solution clearly demonstrated the advantage of being able to use standard commodity hardware.

In 2002, Shiratuddin and Thabet [15] described the implementation of a virtual office walkthrough system based on the Unreal Engine. They derived the geometry from 2D CAD data importing it into the engine. Furthermore they used cheap input devices like the Microsoft Sidewinder Freestyle Pro gamepad in conjunction with the engine's real-time capabilities to allow 6-DOF real-time interaction in a photo-realistic environment. Most of the data conversion was either executed manually or using commercial tools. In our own research, presented in the following sections, we tried to automate the process as much as possible.

Germanchis et al. [8, 9] explored 2004 the potential of game technology for the visualization of geographical data in the context of human path finding and spatial cognition research.

The visual quality and the level of interaction provided by modern game engines had certainly reached a level making them suitable for research in the area of human cognition. The authors used a full set of professional commercial tools, e.g. ArcGIS, to prepare the data for the game engine. This again contrasts our own (semi-)automatic approaches.

Fritsch and Kada [7] discussed 2004 indoor as well as outdoor visualization of geographical data based on different game engines, among them the Quake3 Engine and the Unreal Engine 2. They also discussed the benefits of game engines compared to other software libraries and presented concepts for integrating them with other software packages for different purposes, e.g. Computer Aided Facility Management-Systems. They came to the conclusion that the conversion process of geographical data into the data format of the game engine is one of the major obstacles for every game engine based application.

Arendash [2] demonstrated 2004 how the Unreal editor could be exploited as an intuitive authoring tool for web-based virtual worlds, i.e. VRML or X3D based virtual worlds. He presented a tool to extract geometry, texturing, and lighting data from the Unreal data format into a valid VRML/X3D representation.

Also in 2004, Lepouras and Vassilakis [12] presented the concept of building virtual museums by using a game engine. This virtual exhibition space took advantage of the high visual quality of modern game engines. Lepouras and Vassilakis also conducted a user acceptance study of their virtual museum prototype, which showed very promising results.

In 2005, Jacobson and Lewis [11] presented an open source project derived from the Unreal Engine called CaveUT for immersive Cave-like virtual reality projection environments. In the same year, Stock et al. [16] demonstrated how the Torque Game Engine can be connected to a web-based map server to create an easy-to-use collaborative environment for landscape visualization and planning. They exploited not only the rendering capabilities, but especially the networking features present in most computer game engines.

In other works, game engines have also been used to provide visualization and interaction metaphors in completely different and more abstract areas, which are not listed here because they would go beyond the scope of this paper.

3 Projects at the Welfenlab

This section will report on three projects, realized with students of the Welfenlab. The first is a (very basic) visualization of caves with Quake3. A second approach with Unreal Tournament 2004 had the same goal. The third project focused on landscape visualization in planing processes with FarCry.

The base for the first two projects was a digital model of man-made caves, which we reconstructed before in a previous work. Its original goal was to receive a reconstruction as precise as possible, resulting in a highly detailed triangle surface, which could also be exported as a solid volume model for CAD applications like AutoCAD.

3.1 Cave Visualization with Quake3

The first approach to visualize the reconstructed caves in a first person perspective used the (even at that time) rather old Quake3. The main reason for this was that Quake3 was well understood and available for Windows and Linux. Quake3 was produced and published by IdSoftware, released in December 1999 and supported shaders, curved surfaces, 32-bit color and of course hardware rendering. Only a single license (of the original game) was necessary for the presentation of the results.

The goal of this first project was not only to see if it is possible to visualize the cave, but also to analyze how difficult it would be to convert our high resolutional scientific data into the restricted surface representation of a computer game, without losing too many details. This work was done by Dominik Sarnow in his junior thesis. The choice of the game engine was based on the following criteria:

- the engine must support dynamic light computations
- it should have no license conflicts
- it should use an open file format that is easy to understand
- it should have at least some available documentation

Quake3 fulfilled all but the third criterion, because as almost all other game engines, the native Quake3 level format is binary, proprietary and far from being human readable. Fortunately, there was an easy solution for this: the existence of the level editor GtkRadiant.

GtkRadiant is a level editor for Quake3 and other games. It is free for non-commercial use and is available for several platforms. Its native map format is a sequence of numbered entities, the first entity always being the world which contains geometrical objects (brushes). An entity consists of a class name, an origin that defines the place of the entity in the map and texture/material properties.

Instead of writing a converter of our data into the binary format of Quake3, we decided to export into the text format of GtkRadiant. Still we had to deal with the specific restrictions of Quake3: a limited number of triangles (per level), a map format that can only interpret convex objects and most obvious: all coordinates had to be of integer value.

Since the maximal number of triangles was limited, a prestep reducing the numbers of triangles was necessary. We used a simple shortest-edge removal procedure which was easy to implement and produced acceptable results.

The geometry supported by GtkRadiant consisted of planar and convex geometric entities, *cut out* of a plane. Since our original data was a triangulated surface, the natural approach seemed to be to turn each triangle into a map entity. However, this resulted in a huge number of entities, consequently we spent the extra effort of locating planar areas in our original surface and finding suitable compositions of convex polygons, reducing the number of entities significantly. This interesting geometrical problem was looked into more deeply in the bachelor's thesis of Daniela Lauer.

The problem of transferring vertex coordinates to integer was easy to solve: center the cave data, scale the coordinates (taking into account that the maximum supported integer value for a coordinate is 64k) and delete extra decimal places. Afterwards a correction step was necessary to remove degenerated triangles. Due to the nature of the internal geometry description, it was very important to create closed surfaces, because otherwise the number of polygons in the resulting level file exploded.

Fig. 2 Walking through the reconstructed cave with Quake3

In the resulting *Quake3 level*, colored light sources were placed at the exact positions of the lasers during the measuring of the original caves, giving a very intuitive impression of the visibility region of each measurement, shown in figure 2.

3.2 Cave Visualization with UT 2004

During the work with Quake3, we realized that the visual restrictions would be quite strong, resulting in a second project using the more modern game Unreal Tournament 2004 (UT 2004), leading to the bachelor's thesis of Michael Hanel.

In the UT 2004 project, we followed a similar approach: writing a converter that would not export to the (proprietary and binary) format of the game itself, but into the text format of its level editor, which is free for download.

The Unreal Engine 2 was designed for PC, Sony PlayStation2 and Microsoft XBox and runs with Microsoft Windows XP and Linux. It was used in Unreal Tournament 2004 and Unreal 2. It supports CSG (constructive solid geometry) and BSP (binary space partitioning) geometry, 12 steps of MIP-Mapping, static and dynamic light sources. The texture format is 32 bit with a resolution up to 2048 × 2048 pixels. The engine can show up to 150.000 triangles in view.

Contrary to UT 2004, which also runs on Linux, the map editor UnrealEd 3.0 is a Windows-based application. It can read and write two native data formats: *Unreal Tournament Map .ut2* (binary) and *Unreal Text Format .t3d* (plain). Within the editor, every object is represented by an *Actor*. *Actor* objects combine general and specific attributes, such as the object class, position, size, color, etc. The most important actor classes are *Brushes*, *TriggerLights* (Lights) and the *PlayerStart*.

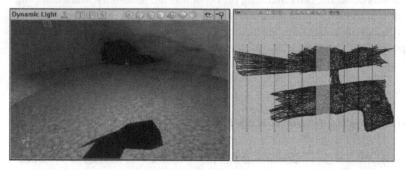

Fig. 3 BSP Holes and their solution: segmenting the surface into several brushes

One of the biggest problems in this work was that the original data consisted of several thousand triangles for the cave surface, producing high computing costs for the engine. The first approach was to convert the whole cave as a single brush object, which turned out to be problematic, since the resulting level contained BSP holes. Therefore we had to reduce the number of triangles per brush. Experiments showed that 500 triangles per brush seemed to be an upper limit.

In the bachelor's thesis of Michael Hanel, this was solved by an equidistant segmentation of the original data into horizontal slices, illustrated in figure 3. These segments were converted into brushes that needed to be closed with side walls for the automated merging within the engine. The equidistant segmentation approach was not optimal, since it did not guarantee an upper limit of triangles per brush, but relatively easy to implement and chosen due to time constraints.

The restriction of 500 triangles per brush cannot be taken for granted, it just appeared to reduce the BSP holes (almost) to zero, which we found out experimentally. In all three projects, similar engine limitations turned out during development

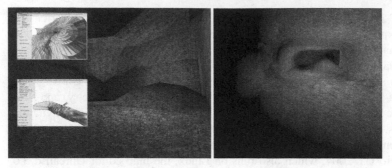

Fig. 4 A screen shot showing the UT 2004 version of the cave in the level editor and the game itself

and had to be analyzed with trial-and-error methods. This seems to be a common problem for *Serious Gaming* projects, as described in section 4.

After this was done, the last remaining problem was the lack of a texture mapping method, that would provide the cave walls with a sufficiently realistic appearance. Together with dynamic lighting, the result was very convincing as seen in figure 4, giving people not involved in the project the immediate impression of a natural cave, much more than in the former Quake3 visualization.

3.3 Landscape Visualization with FarCry

The third project we want to describe in this paper focuses on landscape visualization and planning (cf. [10]). Its main goal is to apply the visualization and interaction capabilities of modern game engines, in this case the CryEngine, to build the prototype of a visualization tool for landscape architects. Our goal was to provide a tool that generates a quick but photo-realistic visualization of an area based on real geographical data, allowing interactive movement through the landscape and real-time interactive modification of the terrain layout and vegetation placement.

One possible usage scenario could be a landscape architect, having a meeting with customers and trying to present his ideas and how they will transfer into reality. Many people have difficulties to imagine how the look of a landscape might change, e.g. with different arrangements of trees and other plants, therefore it is often crucial to provide images or models of the target outcome. This can be a very time consuming and expensive process. Under these circumstances the use of game engines might help to reduce the cost, when compared to professional solutions, while at the same time enhancing the visual quality of the final images. Game Engines also provide the opportunity for collaborative, interactive walkthroughs with no or very low additional cost.

A crucial requirement for a landscape planning tool is the possibility of fast modifications of the terrain and of the placement and arrangement of the vegetation and other objects. This poses an additional challenge in comparison to 'simple' visualization tasks. In section 1 we argued that one major benefit of computer game technology is the optimization for commodity hardware. This was also a major concern in this project because in our scenario a landscape architect would have to be able to use his standard desktop or notebook computer to run our tool in front of his customers.

The CryEngine [4] is a commercial game engine developed by Crytek. It was first employed in the game Farcry, which we used for this project. The engine itself is accompanied by an editor tool called CryEngine Sandbox [3].

Our overall approach can be described as follows. In the first step, very similar to the Quake 2 and UT 2004 project, the geographical data is converted into a format that can be read by the CryEngine Sandbox. In the second step, the real-time editing features of the Sandbox are then exploited to perform any necessary modifications or rearrangements or to try out different landscape scenarios. Finally, a map is generated from within the Sandbox that can be used directly by the game, e.g. for collaborative exploration. It is important to note, that we try to automate the conversion process as much as possible to provide landscape architects with an easy to use tool. The key idea is, that the landscape architect only provides the basic data files and the visualization is then boot-strapped by the conversion tool.

Fig. 5 The CryEngine Sandbox [3] is automatically installed together with the game and free for non-commercial use. It provides real-time interactive tools for terrain shaping and vegetation placement.

We decided to employ the CryEngine because it supports very large outdoor terrains, naturally an important point in our application. The CryEngine Sandbox has also been a key factor. In contrast to many other editing tools, the Sandbox provides real-time interactive editing and a very comprehensive set of tools for terrain shaping and vegetation placement. It also supports seamless switching between in-game and editor modes (figure 5).

Our terrain visualization and the automatic placement of vegetation is based on two types of data. First, we need a digital elevation model (DEM), which describes the general shape of the landscape to a degree limited by the resolution of the available DEM. Second, we need a segmentation of the terrain according to types of vegetation present in the respective areas to be visualized. This segmentation usually decomposes the landscape into areas like forest, field, or meadow. For the purpose of storing the segmentation we used ESRI shape files [5], which is a standard data format commonly used in geographic information systems.

Fig. 6 Ground Texture vs. Aerial Photography. The generated ground texture and the aerial photography of the same area match very well even though we used a coarse segmentation.

We have tested out prototype with sample data from certain areas in Lower Saxony and have received some very convincing results concerning realism and visual quality, shown in figure 6.

The biggest difficulties we encountered during the project were connected to the data conversion process. The resolution of the DEMs is in general very different compared to the internal heightmap resolution used in the game engine. Therefore this data needs to be resampled to be used by the Sandbox. The shape file data has to be matched and positioned correctly onto the terrain and of course it has to be clipped accordingly. Finally, the file formats used by the CryEngine are not publicly documented.

4 Reflection

In the last section, we presented three approaches to use existing computer game technology in scientific applications. The question that remains is: Was it a good idea or would it have been more suitable to use professional visualization software? The answer is as usual: *It depends*.

Using commercial computer games for a non-gaming context has huge advantages. First of all, they usually bring state-of-the-art graphics, often supporting a client/server concept which can be used for multi-user applications. Their most important advantage is of course the price: a single license usually does not cost more than 100 US$, while professional visualization tools easily cross 10,000 US$ per copy. Also, the professional software usually requires professional hardware, while computer games are designed to run on last year's low budget PC as well.

However, every advantage comes with a trade-off. The problems of the three projects from the last section seem to be exemplary for the field of *Serious Gaming* and can be divided into four categories:

1. **Lack of documentation**

   No matter how good a game engine and its editors are documented and how large its community is, it seems to be impossible to find out concrete numbers, e.g. the maximum number of polygons per object or the maximum file size of a level. The process of writing tools that convert scientific data into the file format of a game engine (or for its level editor) is usually very experimental.

2. **Engine-Dependent Restrictions**

   As seen in all three projects, every game engine had very specific restrictions, for example the 'integer-coordinates-only' drawback of Quake3 (section 3.1) or the maximum number of triangles per brushes in UT 2004 (section 3.2. These restrictions are usually not obvious before the development starts and result in time-expensive workarounds.

3. **Short Life-Span**

   Computer hardware evolves fast and a modern computer game usually lasts only a few years. As long as it is new, it is usually supported well, but compared to professional animation software, it is very unlikely that it will run on future operating systems or on hardware that will come out 3-4 years after its launch.

4. **Not Extendable**

   The application can do what the game can do. Nothing more, nothing less. Future customer requests might be expensive or impossible to implement.

So why is it still reasonable to continue the work with game engines? Because of their potential. Computer games are highly specialized but also highly optimized, with development costs matching those of Hollywood movies. These games are sold at a very reasonable price as they are produced for a mass market. The situation can be compared with the current run on GPU-Programming. It can be safely said that (ab)using the GPU for non-rendering purposes is a very unpleasant if not questionable way of writing programs. Yet the impressive speedup that is gained with additional hardware costs of zero (almost every computer already has a fast GPU) made it very popular.

If the scientific application matches the potential of a game engine close enough, as in the use of FarCry for visualizing landscape planning processes, the costs of developing software with similar capabilities would by far go beyond the costs of finding solutions for the engine restrictions or buying a professional software. As long as the original problem does not exceed the capabilities too much, it might always be worth a closer look. However, one should always keep the drawbacks mentioned above in mind.

5 Summary and Outlook

In this work we reported on three different visualization projects making use of 3D computer games and tried to classify them in the context of other *Serious Gaming* projects (sections 2 and 3). We have shown that the visualization of scientific data with game engines is possible and leads to promising results. We also discussed its drawbacks (section 4) and tried to extract common problems of all three projects.

In the future we would like to extend the presented work. Firstly, we would like to incorporate the latest developments in the area of game technology, i.e. enhanced rendering methods and the like. Secondly, we would like to explore the full potential of game engines not only in graphical terms. We think there is a great potential in using the available artificial intelligence and networking capabilties of modern engines.

References

1. Abt, C.C.: Serious Games. University Press of America (1987)
2. Arendash, D.: The unreal editor as a web 3d authoring environment. In: Proceedings of the ninth international conference on 3D Web technology, pp. 119–126. ACM, Monterey, California (2004)
3. Crytek GmbH: CryEngine Sandbox Far Cry Edition User Manual, 1.1 edn. (2004)
4. Crytek GmbH: Far Cry Engine Overview, 1.0 edn. (2005)
5. Environmental Systems Research Institute: ESRI Shapefile Technical Description (1998). White Paper
6. Freudenberg, B., Masuch, M., Röber, N., Strothotte, T.: The computer-visualistik-raum: Veritable and inexpensive presentation of a virtual reconstruction. VAST2001: Virtual Reality, Archaelogy, and Cultural Heritage (2001)
7. Fritsch, D., Kada, M.: Visualisation using game engines. Archiwum ISPRS **35** (2004)
8. Germanchis, T., Cartwright, W.: The potential to use games engines and games software to develop interactive, three-dimensional visualisations of geography. ICC Proceedings, Durban pp. 352–357 (2003)
9. Germanchis, T., Pettit, C., Cartwright, W.: Building a three-dimensional geospatial virtual environment on computer gaming technology: Geographic visualization. Journal of spatial science **49**, 89–95 (2004)
10. Herwig, A., Paar, P.: Game engines: Tools for landscape visualization and planning? Trends in GIS and Virtualization in Environmental Planning and Design (2002)
11. Jacobson, J., Lewis, M.: Game engine virtual reality with caveut. Computer **38**, 79–82 (2005)
12. Lepouras, G., Vassilakis, C.: Virtual museums for all: employing game technology for edutainment. Virtual Reality **8**, 96–106 (2004)
13. Rhyne, T.M.: Computer games and scientific visualization. Commun. ACM **45**, 40–44 (2002)
14. Sawyer, B.: Serious games: Broadening games impact beyond entertainment. Computer Graphics Forum **26**, xviii (2007)
15. Shiratuddin, M.F., Thabet, W.: Virtual office walkthrough using a 3d game engine. International Journal of Design Computing **4**, 1329–7147 (2002)
16. Stock, C., Bishop, I.D., O'Connor, A.: Generating virtual environments by linking spatial data processing with a gaming engine. Trends in Real-time Landscape Visualization and Participation, Proceedings at Anhalt University of Applied Sciences, Wichmann pp. 324–329 (2005)
17. Zyda, M.: From visual simulation to virtual reality to games. Computer **38**, 25–32 (2005)

An Interactive Visual Canon Platform

Mathias Funk and Christoph Bartneck

Abstract The canon is a composition pattern with a long history and many forms. The concept of the canon has also been applied to experimental film making and on Japanese television. We describe our work-in-progress on an Interactive Visual Canon Platform (IVCP) that enables creators of visual canons to design their movements through rapid cycles of performance and evaluation. The IVCP system provides real time support for the actors; they can see the canon resulting from their movements while they are still performing. We describe some possible approaches to a solution, and reasons for choosing the approach that we have implemented. The hardware has reached a stable state, but we are still optimizing the visual processing of the system. A first user test is planned to provide us with information for improving the system.

1 Introduction

In music, a canon is a composition employing one or more repetitions of a melody, played with a certain delay [3]. The initial melody is called the leader, and the imitative melody is called the follower. The follower must be based on the leader by being either an exact replication or a transformation of the leader. Several types of canon are possible, including the simple canon, the interval canon, the crab canon, the table canon, and the mensuration canon. Two well-known examples of a simple canon are "Row, Row, Row Your Boat" and "Frère Jacques".

Mathias Funk
Department of Electrical Engineering, Eindhoven University of Technology, Netherlands, e-mail: m.funk@tue.nl

Christoph Bartneck
Department of Industrial Design, Eindhoven University of Technology, Netherlands, e-mail: c.bartneck@tue.nl

Please use the following format when citing this chapter:

Funk, M. and Bartneck, C., 2008, in IFIP International Federation for Information Processing, Volume 279; *New Frontiers for Entertainment Computing*; Paolo Ciancarini, Ryohei Nakatsu, Matthias Rauterberg, Marco Roccetti; (Boston: Springer), pp. 23–32.

Fig. 1 Canon by Norman McLaren.

Experimental film maker Norman McLaren introduced the concept of the canon to the visual arts and, in 1965, received the Canadian Film Award for his movie "Canon" [2]. This movie can be considered a visual canon. The actor enters the picture to perform a certain movement in his role as the leader. After the completion of this "voice" he walks forward. A copy of himself, the "follower", enters the picture and repeats this movement while the leader introduces another movement. This process continues until four copies of the same actor, "voices", are present on the screen (see Figure 1). McLaren continues with variations of this canon by introducing transformations, such as mirroring. Instead of walking on the stage, the "mirror" voice now walks on the ceiling. Moreover, he introduces causal relationships between the voices. One voice, for example, might kick a second voice. This is particularly interesting if the two voices are walking backwards. Then the relationships are also introduced in the reversed time sequence. First the leader performs the receiving of the kick before he moves on to perform the actual kick. The voices can also have a spatial relationship; while one voice bends down, a second may swing its arms.

More recently, the comedy duo Itsumo Kokokara, consisting of Kazunari Yamada and Hidenori Kikuchi, has included the performance of a visual canon as part of the daily show "Pythagoras Switch" on the Japanese National television channel NHK. As in McLarens movie, followers imitated the movements of the leader. The duo named their visual canon "Algorithm March". It is constrained to the format of a simple canon in which no variations or transformations are introduced by the followers. They invited different groups of followers into their dance performance. Prominent followers have included the NHK news team, the Japanese Polar Research team, Sonys Qrio robots, and many more.

The creation of a new visual canon is very difficult, since a whole team needs to study the specific sequence of new movements. Only when all actors perform the canon correctly, can the design of it as a whole be evaluated. The long duration of each iterative cycle is a major obstacle in the design process of visual canons. In this paper we shall describe our work-in-progress on an interactive visual canon platform (IVCP) that supports the creation of visual canons and that can be used to extend them in real time.

Fig. 2 Interdependency between leader and follower that can only be achieved through a real-time system.

2 Requirements

The IVCP requires a large screen on which the design can be displayed. Naturally, the followers have to be shown life-size (to match the leader - the leader can also be shown on the screen). The Algorithm March uses eight voices, and with an average step distance of around 75 centimeters, a total of 6 meters is needed to display the whole cycle. The screen should therefore be at least 2 meters high and 6 meters wide.

Besides enabling actors to design, learn, and practice new visual canons, the IVCP should also enable a broader audience to experience a visual canon. Arts festivals and exhibitions are ideal events for this, so it is desirable to have a portable system. It follows that the IVCP must be a free-standing structure. It should not have to rely on the availability of walls on which it could be mounted. It should also be possible to assemble and disassemble the IVCP quickly, and the individual components should not be of a size that would make transportation difficult. For example, shipping a six-meter tube would be very impractical.

Needless to say, the IVCP must operate in real time. Simply recording an actor and playing multiple copies of the recording with a time delay would be insufficient. The actor needs to be able to interact with the followers immediately. Only a direct interaction would allow the actor to experiment quickly with movements and gestures. If, for example, the actor wants to take a swing at the follower, then he/she must know exactly where the follower is (see Figure 2). It is also desirable that the IVCP can be controlled without any additional input devices. For example, in Sonys Eye Toy game, the players can control the game with gestures. This gesture control can be the starting point for the IVCPs gesture control.

3 Solution

The key characteristic of a canon is its structural consistency; only the leader has the freedom to perform, the follower(s) must conform to the leader movements with the utmost precision and discipline. Also, when watching the performance of a canon, one realizes that, in principle, each movement is performed at the same position by all the actors (voices) of the canon, one after the other. The algorithm in the solution software takes advantage of the strict algorithmic nature of the canon. In practice, the only degree of freedom in the actors performance lies in the movements of the leader. These are restricted to the forward direction to avoid risk of overlap with the followers.

The solution algorithm includes several delay units that record a short video of the leaders movements, wait a certain amount of time, and project the video back onto the screen. During the waiting period the leader has moved forward, so he/she does not interfere with the playback. Next, the first playback unit is fed into a second delay unit, which records, waits, and plays the video of the first delay unit. This results in two followers appearing on the screen. This chain of feedback units can be extended for as many followers as needed. However, this simple approach works only if the playback is not projected back onto the screen before the leader has left the scene. Otherwise the playback interferes with the recording of the video. Not only the leader, but also the followers would be captured and create their own followers (voices). These voices of voices would populate the screen. They might overlap and cause even more distorted voices. Soon the output is a beautiful, abstract cloud of color, a chaos that contradicts the strict minimalism of the canon. It becomes clear that the major challenge is to control the feedback. The followers must be based only on the leader. There are several possible approaches to singling out the original (human) leader by masking out the rest of the recorded picture, including all the projected followers, thus breaking the infinite feedback loops and enabling the system to work as intended.

The first approach we tried was to subtract the projected video from the captured video. The resulting difference picture would not contain the newly added followers, but only the leader. Since, we already know what to project (the followers), it should have been possible to use this picture as a mask to isolate the leader. At first sight, this solution appears simple and elegant. However, it turned out to be very difficult to align the recorded video with the projected video. In the first place, the known video that is to be projected is not the same as what is ultimately shown on the screen because of the optical properties of the camera that records this video and the projector itself. The camera can never be placed in the exact same position as the projector, and this will always result in slight optical discrepancies. Secondly, the two videos must be aligned not only in space but also in time. The projection and recording process takes a certain amount of time. The video that is fed back into the computer is slightly delayed relative to its original. The geometric and temporal alignment of the projected image with the recorded video proved to be difficult to control, which led to unreliable results. Therefore a more robust solution was needed, since the system should be usable in all kinds of different demonstration environments.

Another approach would be to place an additional camera behind the projection screen. This second camera would record only the shadow of the leader, because he/she is the only body that can possibly cast a shadow on the screen. An alternative to this idea could have been to place an infra-red camera next to the projector. The infra-red camera would isolate the leader using his/her heat signature. Both approaches would require additional cameras that would need to be calibrated in space and time against the original setup. Adding these components would increase the complexity of the system and introduce additional sources of errors that would have a negative impact on the systems reliability.

A solution that works with only one camera and projector is preferable. One option would be to use visual cues. For example, the position of each follower could be indicated with visual markers, such as cropping crosses, that can be recognized easily by the image processing algorithm. It would then be easy to mask out the followers from the recorded video. Since the visual cues would be added in the rendering of the previous iteration, they are part of the projected picture and therefore perfectly aligned with the followers. However, visual cues may distract the observer, and would have a negative impact on the overall aesthetics. They would not only clutter the screen, but they would also distract the attention of the observer from the performance. Instead of enjoying the performance, the observer might focus on the artifacts of the technical implementation.

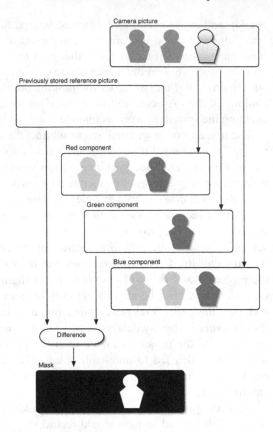

Fig. 3 Color separation for masking the leader.

For our final solution, we took the concept of visual cues to the next level. We integrated the visual cues into the underlying concept of the performance: the first follower projected by the system is displayed in a light green color that is easily recognizable by the image processing system. It then becomes unnecessary to hide the markers since they are visually appealing and become part of the performance. This principle means that if the leader looks back he/she will see only moving "shadows". One by one the projected green shapes revert to the recorded picture of the leader, providing a natural and smooth transition from bare "shadows" to real followers.

What first comes to mind is the chroma key technique [1], commonly used in the movie industry. Light green items, including the background, can be substituted by other film material in the post-processing phase. For example, the movie "300" used this method extensively. All the actors were filmed against a light green background that was replaced, in the post production, with a computer rendering of ancient Greece. Light green is one of the colors that least resembles human skin tone, and can therefore be substituted without making the person on screen look like an alien. Using this "green-screen" technique, the system could mask the area behind the leader and avoid the unacceptable feedback cycle mentioned earlier. The chroma key technique would not be sufficiently robust to withstand changes in the physical environment such as the size of the demonstration room, the lighting, or the properties of the projector. Instead we basically exploit the color separation of the RGB video. The leader performs in front of a pure white background, and the green color of the followers is so light that it is very close to white if seen only in the green component of the RGB video. Figure 3 illustrates this principle, showing a moment at which the camera sees the leader and two light-green followers. The green component of the color separation shows only the leader, while the red and blue components show small traces of the followers, because the green first projected and then recorded might not be as pure as intended due to the factors explained above. This does not matter as long as the green is light enough to appear as white in the green color component, so that the followers merge with the white background of the screen, and only the shape of the leader remains. To build a mask from this picture it is necessary to subtract a white reference picture from the green channel. This reference picture can be captured before the performance. The complete processing chain is as follows. First a masking component uses visual cues to mask the whole screen except for the picture of the leader. The resulting image, which is mostly black, is then fed into several delay units that "clone" the followers. All cloned pictures are then combined, and visual cues are set accordingly. Finally the picture is projected onto the screen.

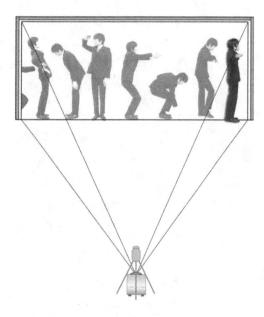

Fig. 4 Model of the IVCP setup.

4 Realization

Given the portability requirement for the system, and the solution algorithm described above, the IVCP can be implemented with a single camera and a single projector (see Figure 4). This eliminates the need to align and synchronize multiple screens and cameras. Otherwise, this difficult and lengthy procedure would have to be repeated every time the system was moved. Full HD cameras and projectors have recently entered the market at a reasonable price. They have a resolution of 1920 x 1080 pixels, which means that they have a 16:9 aspect ratio [4]. The projection screen should be optimized for this aspect ratio, meaning a height of 3.37 meters to achieve the required 6 meter width. However, even tall people rarely exceed 2 meters in height. We therefore decided to exclude one third of the vertical dimension, which resulted in final dimensions for the screen of 592 cm x 222 cm. It follows that the projection will use 1920 x 720 pixels. The Optoma HD80 projector that we used had to be placed at a distance of 14 meters from the screen to achieve this projection size.

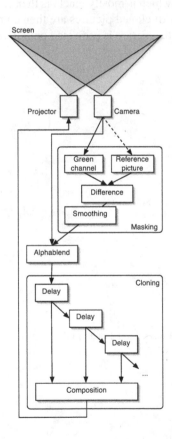

Fig. 5 System architecture.

The hardware for image projection and capture is connected to a computer running Mac OS X and Max/MSP, and Cycling74s graphical development environment for music and multimedia, together with the video processing sub system Jitter. This provides a convenient basis for rapid prototyping of the IVCP algorithm, and also results in a system that is easy to extend with additional components for gesture or audio control.

Figure 5 shows an essential part of the system architecture. In order to give a proper overview and to hide over-complex parts, several details of the algorithm have been omitted. The camera provides a picture of the screen which is fed into three different blocks. The first block simply stores a reference picture of the empty screen taken before the start of the performance. The second block extracts the green channel from the RGB video stream.

As described in section 3, Solution, a difference picture is created and, after some further smoothing, is blended with the live image in the third block, using the alpha channel. This subsystem incorporates all masking functionality. The isolated image of the leader must be cloned to obtain followers. This is the purpose of the next processing stage: the video is fed into a delay component that simply stores the data and outputs it after a certain predefined amount of time. As explained in the Solution section, this process of storing and delayed playback is repeated several times. The output of each delay unit is a layer containing one follower picture. In order to project the followers together on the screen, these layers must be merged.

5 Conclusions

The hardware of the system has been built and tested, but the biggest challenge was to find a room large enough to set up the system. It turned out that positioning the projector and camera at the same height is not only important for image alignment, but also for minimizing the amount of shadow captured. (Since a mostly white image is projected, any three?dimensional object in front of the white screen casts a strong shadow.) As long as projector and camera are at the same height this does not matter much, but increased vertical separation will result in a bigger shadow being captured by the camera, which is hard to remove using image processing.

Our next steps will be to provide improvements in the performance, visual appearance, and general robustness of the system. The capture and processing of a Full HD video in real time pushes the processing power of currently available personal computers to its limits, but, especially for user testing, the system should be capable of sustained stable activity. Participants facing a user test will include those who already know about the canon as well as those who are encountering the concept for the first time. Additionally, it is crucial to keep the image processing core modular and reusable, something which also affects the robustness of the system architecture. Future work will deal with integrating audio control, music, and a comprehensive gesture interface. Most importantly the user test will produce further requirements for system improvements. Later on we might think of more sophisticated visual effects or special guidance for first-time users. Moreover, game-like attributes can be added to the system, e.g. different levels of canon complexity, obstacles, and moving objects that must be used in the performance.

Generally, the approach taken looks promising and could probably lead to a new kind of entertainment experience that would not only encourage full body interaction, but also support the development of mental skills as well as body control and especially the connection between the two.

References

1. Jack, K. (2004). Video demystified: a handbook for the digital engineer (4th ed.). Oxford Burlington, MA: Newnes.
2. McLaren, N. (Writer) (2006). Norman McLaren: The Masters Edition: Homevision.
3. Norden, H. (1982). The Technique of Canon: Branden Books.
4. Weise, M. and Weynand, D. (2004). How Video Works: Focal Press Boston.

Physical Emotion Induction and Its Use in Entertainment: Lessons Learned

Ralph Kok+, Joost Broekens*

*Telematica Instituut

Enschede, The Netherlands

+Media Technology / *LIACS

Leiden University, Leiden, The Netherlands

Abstract It is well known that our emotional response is related to our bodily state, and more specifically that our bodily state can directly influence particular emotions we feel. It appears, however, that this fact has so far not had a significant influence in the entertainment industry. We first review existing work on physical emotion induction. Based on this work we present several techniques to influence emotional responses through physical means in a non-cognitive manner. The basis for the different techniques is a two-factor model of emotion: Pleasure and Arousal. We selected 4 sets of movie clips that correspond to the 4 possible quadrants existing in the 2 factor model. We have implemented some of the emotion induction techniques in a physical device (interactive chair) and tested the effects on the immersiveness of the movie clips and the emotional experience of the participants.

Introduction

Humans can be emotionally influenced in many ways. The entertainment industry makes good use of this fact by using video and audio to do so. We see a film and are grabbed by the story, we hear happy, sad or tense music and our feelings respond accordingly. There is a multitude of audiovisual means to influence our emotions, but somehow, emotion induction through *physical* means has been largely ignored, even though psychological research clearly shows that our emotional state is at least partially dependent on our physical state. Examples of devices that do use physical means, such as vibrating game controllers and moving seats in amusement park theatres, mostly mimic what is seen on the screen to enhance the experience and make it more immersive. They work well in achieving their goal, but they are not aimed at inducing a particular emotion, as music or storylines are.

Please use the following format when citing this chapter:

Kok, R. and Broekens, J., 2008, in IFIP International Federation for Information Processing, Volume 279; *New Frontiers for Entertainment Computing*; Paolo Ciancarini, Ryohei Nakatsu, Matthias Rauterberg, Marco Roccetti; (Boston: Springer), pp. 33–48.

Here we report on research that aims to influence a person's emotions through physical means, in order to enhance the emotions experienced while watching a movie or playing a video game. To enhance rather than disrupt such an immersive experience, this process of physical emotion elicitation should happen implicitly, i.e., without the user being cognitively aware of any influence. Furthermore, we try to minimize invasiveness of the mechanisms used to achieve emotion elicitation.

We first review the concept of emotion, its relation with the bodily state, and physical emotion induction. Based on this review we present different techniques to influence particular emotions, and discuss an experiment with a physical device that implements some of these techniques. Emotional influence through audio and video is ignored in this research as it does not involve direct *physical* influence.

The Nature of Emotion

Emotion has long been the terrain of much research and discussion. Ever since James [1] presented a theory stating that emotions are only the result of changes in the body, the roles played by physiology and cognition in relation to emotion have been heavily debated. The current views on these relationships are described by Philippot et al. [2] in three models, the most interesting of which, for this research, is the *central network model*. This model argues that different emotions are associated with different changes in body state, and that changes in body state that are typical for a specific emotion will elicit that emotion and that this phenomenon, called *peripheral feedback*, occurs at an implicit level (i.e., without the person experiencing it being explicitly aware of the process). We focus on this model, as it is the most relevant in the context of implicit physical emotion induction.

Influencing Emotion

Facial expression   It has been shown that facial expression can increase feelings of emotion [3, 4]. What is more, emotion-inducing facial expressions have been shown to be specific for specific emotions. However, physically forcing someone to have a certain facial expression in order to enhance emotional sensation is, arguably, not a good way to enhance entertainment in an unobtrusive way.

Posture   The findings for emotion induction through facial expressions were hypothesized to be true for postures as well. The results of a second experiment in Duclos et al.'s research suggest that this is indeed the case, This study revealed that in some cases specific postures can be associated to fear, anger and sadness.

In earlier research, Riskind & Gotay [5] showed developed helplessness and stress reactions in response to posture manipulations. They showed that stress reactions can in fact occur simultaneously with a slumped-over posture, as long as an external factor explaining the emotional response is present. In the context of physical emotion induction in entertainment, this point is of great importance, because while for example one is watching a movie, an external factor would indeed be present to explain any experienced emotional response and physical posture manipulation may be used to enhance the emotional experience triggered by the audiovisual media as long as the manipulation occurs without the user being aware of it.

Respiration   While Boiten et al. [6] had already found objective respiratory patterns that could be associated with specific emotions and Philippot et al. [2] showed that people can produce quite specific emotions through self-regulation of breathing patterns. These patterns were subjective, but specific, showed a clear differentiation among emotions and were consistent with the objective patterns that were found by Boiten et al.. The subjective breathing patterns found in the first study were used in a second study to induce emotions in subjects who were unaware of the goal of the study and simply followed breathing instructions.

Temperature   It has been shown that temperatures of parts of the body vary in association with emotions [7, 8, 9]. McFarland has shown a relation between skin temperature changes and affect in music. The causal relationship in this case is inferred in the direction of emotion towards physical response. A reversed causal effect where skin temperature changes can cause changes in affect would be of great interest for the purposes of implicit emotion elicitation.

Such a relation has been investigated, but most investigations on this subject focus on the relation between temperature and aggression (for a review, see Anderson [10]). The basic hypothesis concerning this relation is that uncomfortably hot temperatures increase aggressive tendencies. Although findings are not fully consistent across various studies, especially not for those performed in a laboratory setting, results do clearly support the temperature-aggression hypothesis. An increase in general negative affect as a result of hot as well as cold temperatures has more recently been shown by Anderson et al. [11], but this increase was considerably less pronounced than the effect of temperature on hostility.

Haptic and Tactile Feedback   In the context of video games, haptic feedback is implemented through vibrating controllers, often mimicking sound effects or other events seen on screen. It can also be used to communicate information, for example in wearable tactile displays [12]. Some interesting experiments have been performed that use haptic feedback in the communication of emotion between humans, but they are concerned with active cognitive interpretation of a communicated emotional state [13, 14, 15]. None of these implementations are used to elicit an emotional state in a user though.

More interestingly, a product called the Hapticat was developed to study the relationship between touch and affect [16]. The product can be described as an abstract pet, communicating emotional states through various behaviors. While people were able to discern distinct emotions and the interaction changed their personal affect, the results are ambiguous when considering this for use in implicit emotion induction. Users were presented with a variety of emotions to ascribe to the 'pet', making them cognitively aware to the presence of an emotional charge. Also, the experiment did not seem to be aimed at reproducing the same emotions in the users through for example empathy, but rather influenced users' affect in terms of elation and surprise when the pet responded.

Heart rate   Tactile feedback can be used to in a more specifically emotion inductive manner, namely to influence heart rate. Research indicates that false feedback of heart rate has the potential to alter our emotional response [17, 18, 19], even when the feedback signal is ignored [20]. Although most studies do not show that false feedback of heart rate influences actual heart rate, they do show that emotional interpretation itself can change as a result of false feedback. Whether it works through a process of attribution or through a more direct and purely physical process is beyond the scope of this research to answer. What is important here is the existence of an effect.

Palmar sweat   Let's now look at the phenomenon of the sweaty palm. It has been shown that skin conductance changes in response to emotion [21, 22, 23, 24, 25, 26]. Anxiety or emotional arousal affects the resistance and conductance of the skin: the higher the level of arousal, the higher the electrical conductance and the lower the resistance of the skin. The activity of the sweat glands has been associated with this effect, and is generally accepted as an index for the level of arousal [27, 28]. Of course in this research, it is not measurement of anxiety that is of importance, but rather the induction of it. And even though no research to date has investigated emotional responses as a result rather than a cause of palmar sweat, such an implementation deserves attention. A practical advantage here is that Allen et al. [29] have shown that emotional sweating is not restricted to palms, but occurs on other parts of the body as well.

Scent   Odours can have a strong influence on emotion and mood. In fact, this influence can be stronger than that of any other sense, due to a more direct linkage of the olfactory sense with the part in our brain that is "critical for emotional memory" [30, 31]. The result is that odours can get certain meanings and evoke emotional associations, influencing our mood, emotion and performance. Epple & Herz have shown this to be true for children who had learned to associate a certain smell with failure and Rétiveau et al. [32] showed an effect of fine fragrances on the mood of women. The keenness of our sense of smell has been further demonstrated by Haviland-Jones and McGuire [33], who showed that humans can in fact discern the emotions of fear and happiness from body odour. However, due to pratical issues we leave scent out of the equation in this research.

Components of Emotion

How can we induce emotion through physical means and on an implicit level and what representation of emotion should be used?

One approach to answer this question would be to list the specific emotions that have been found to allow for physical elicitation. Such a list would presently consist of fear, anger, sadness and joy. A problem would occur when we try to determine which physical measures can induce which emotions, because not all types of influence mentioned yield distinct results in terms of which emotions they address.

To avoid having to list emotions together with feedback effect, we opted for a different approach. We couple various physical feedback measures to the pleasure-activation model of emotion, as used by Russell [34]. In this model, emotions consist of two dimensions: pleasure and arousal. Any emotion has at least these two components. Based on this model, we have developed ways to use physical measures to influence the emotional state on the pleasure and arousal axis. This approach has the added advantage that we need not achieve the level of specificity used in some researches to achieve one specific emotion. The goal is to stimulate certain emotional responses to enrich an experience in which emotions are already triggered, such as watching a movie. In this setting, manipulation along the two proposed axes should be sufficient to enhance the experienced emotions.

In terms of posture, both fear and anger are very tense, while sadness is related to a very relaxed posture. From this it would seem that posture is most effective in targeting the arousal component of emotion, with high arousal requiring a tense, and low arousal requiring a relaxed posture.

The indicated respiratory patterns for the emotions of joy, anger and sadness are more specific than those for postures even. The aspects that vary among the patterns are speed, amplitude and tenseness of the ribcage and shoulders. The latter is of course more of a posture manipulation. Looking purely at breathing, speed and amplitude remain as important factors, but even though by varying speed and amplitude we can influence emotion, it is unclear in which dimension. It seems that faster, shallower breaths produce high arousal and low pleasure, affecting both dimensions and that slower and deeper breathing reduces arousal, but does not necessarily increase pleasure.

Moving on to temperature, we have seen that aggression can be caused by uncomfortably hot temperatures and negative affect can be induced by hot and cold temperatures alike. Also, the other way around, skin temperature decreases as a result of music with negative affect and increases with positive music. We can conclude, then, that temperature influences the pleasure dimension of emotion when it reaches uncomfortable values, but this may also indicate that comfortable temperatures prevent the occurrence of negative affect and as such, unlike extreme temperatures, may be used in implicit emotion elicitation.

For false haptic heart rate feedback, things are somewhat clearer. By influencing heart rate, we influence arousal.

Then there is palmar sweat, or rather emotional sweat in general. As said, the extent to which the palms of one's hands sweat is an indication for that person's anxiety, which relates to high arousal. Therefore, if sweating can induce an emotional response, it will affect it so that arousal increases.

Practical Implementation

Now that we have an overview of changes in body state that influence emotion, we must look at how they can be implemented. Because we are looking at ways to influence emotion during a multimodal experience, such as watching a movie or playing a video game, modifying a chair to allow for manipulation of a person's body state seems like a logical choice. We now discuss how such a chair could be adapted to implement different emotion induction techniques.

First, it is wise to use a chair with an adjustable angle for the back. This can then be fitted with servomotors for example, making the angle of the back and thus the posture of the person in the chair automatically adjustable.

As easy as it seems to manipulate a person's posture, so hard is it to manipulate a person's breathing pattern. So far, in studies done on the influence of respiratory patterns on emotion, the subjects were asked to actively adjust these patterns. This is something we can not do in the context of what we're trying to achieve, so another way to influence respiration without the person being cognitively aware of it must be found. For now, we have no solutions that do not rely heavily on intuition. In the current experiment, influence of respiration will therefore not be included.

Influence of temperature seems something that should be feasible through an automated system. In a chair, we can think of heating elements and a cooling system integrated into the back and seat of the chair. Another, perhaps more convenient, way may be through the ventilation of air with varying temperatures onto one's neck.

False heartbeat feedback through haptics is something that may be achieved through attaching a set of vibrating units to the legs of the chair; when the frame of a chair vibrates, this will be felt through the entire chair. By measuring the actual heart rate of the person in the chair and adjusting the feedback to be slightly faster or slower, it should be possible to influence the actual heart rate.

As far as sweat goes, inducing or simulating palmar sweat would be ideal, but considering the fact that each person places his or her hands in different locations and positions, inducing sweatiness on a more 'stable' location of the body is much more convenient. In this case the back is a good candidate, as it is at all times resting against the back of the chair and apart from the palms the back is a place where we readily notice sweatiness in response to anxiety. To recreate the experience of a sweaty back, the back of the chair can be fitted with a type of irrigation system which can be triggered to release small droplets of liquid.

Summarized, this gives us the following list of modifications that could be made to the chair:

1. Motors to automatically adjust the back of the chair

2. Ventilation system venting warm or cold air onto the neck of the user and/or heating and cooling elements in the back

3. System for measuring actual heart rate of the user

4. Vibration elements attached to the chair to create heart rate feedback

5. Irrigation system in the back of the chair to moisten the back of the user

Research question

The main question that this research will attempt to answer using this prototype is if physical manipulations can increase the immersiveness of a multimodal experience.

There is much evidence to suggest that physical influence of emotion is possible, supporting the central network model of emotion, and the assumption that more intense emotional reactions to a multimodal experience increase its immersive potential leads to the expectation that the answer to this question will be positive. This leads us to the following hypothesis:

An emotionally charged multimodal experience will be subjectively experienced as being more intense when the physical states related to those emotions are induced than when this is not the case.

To test this hypothesis, we have developed a prototype interactive chair, and tested its effect on the experience subjects have while watching movies clips of different emotional content.

Materials and Methods

Overview   To reduce complexity and duration of development, the prototype chair we developed for this research uses four of the five modes of physical manipulation: posture (1), heart rate (3,4) and temperature (2). See Fig. 1 for a view of the chair. On the left the air flow regulation system can be clearly seen, which consists of tubing connected to a fan at the lower end and opening onto the sides of the participant's neck at the front of the chair. This is used to achieve cooling of the participant to a lower, uncomfortable temperature. Heating is achieved through pads integrated in a flat cushion on the back of the chair. Also on the left picture the vibrating motor can be seen which provides heart rate feedback. It is attached to the back so that vibrations can be felt throughout the entire chair. Automated adjustment of the back for posture manipulation was implemented through an integrated motor. An Arduino I/O board connected to a computer system allowed controlling the hardware of the chair prototype.

Emotional video footage consisting of eight different scenes was shown to a total of 20 participants. The scenes were selected to fall into one of the four quadrants in the pleasure-arousal domain, each quadrant being represented by two scenes. Every participant viewed four scenes without being influenced by the chair and four while the chair attempted active influence, so that for each pleasure-arousal quadrant every person would see one scene with influence and one without. The order of the scenes, as well as which were shown with and without active influence, was randomized for each participant. Each scene was shown to an equal number of participants with and without active influence. To account for a possible need of participants to adjust to the chair being active, the scenes were grouped by influence, meaning that all scenes with influence were shown consecutively, as were those without. Half of the participants started with the scenes with influence, the other half started with those without.

Subjects   The subjects were 10 males and 10 females, aged between 15 and 58 years (mean age 27), 13 of which were students at the Media Technology master programme of Leiden University.

Procedure   The participants, one per session, were led to the experimental setup. They were seated in the chair created for this experiment and faced a computer monitor. The experimenter explained the procedure, took place behind a folding screen and when the participant was ready, the first scene was shown on the computer monitor. After viewing the scene, the participant was presented with a questionnaire, based on the Affective Level Questionnaire [9]. The questions concerning emotions that could be clearly separated into a pleasure and an arousal component were used and intermingled with non-emotional items to obscure the actual goal of the experiment. Two items reflecting the measure of immersion of the participant into the scene were also added. Each question consisted of two terms located at either side of a scale of 1 to 6, 3.5 being the neutral position. A slider could be positioned at 0.1 intervals along the scale to indicate the intensity of the experienced feeling. The questions were slow heartbeat – fast heartbeat, security – anxiety, cold – hot, sadness – joy, contentedness – frustration, distraction – immersion, tired – energetic, boredom – fascination, calmness – tension and unpleasantness – pleasantness. Emotional items were picked to be at opposite sides of the pleasure-arousal domain. One extra question was added: "Try to describe in your own words what emotion(s) you experienced during this scene".

After the participant had answered the questions, the process was repeated until all eight scenes were shown and questionnaires answered. After this, some more questions followed concerning experience with movies, favourite genres, etc. Then the participants were debriefed about the goal of the experiment and had a chance to ask questions and give comments.

Results

Through the questionnaire, each participant rated the intensity of various experienced emotions for each scene. The intensity score reflected which of each set of items was relevant (smaller or larger than 3.5) and how intense it occurred. These values were corrected to reflect the direction and intensity with a number between -1.0 and 1.0 (subtract 3.5, then divide by 3.5).

To analyze the intensity of emotions experienced with and without influence of the chair, the scores for the items reflecting axes in the pleasure-arousal domain were used. The calmness-tension item reflected purely the arousal axis,

Fig. 1. Two views of the chair prototype that was developed for this experiment. On the left the air ventilation system as well as a vibration feedback implementation can be seen. The picture on the right shows the back cushion into which heating pads are integrated and the electronics that communicate with the hardware.

the unpleasantness-pleasantness item the pleasure axis, and sadness-joy and con-
tentedness-frustration two pleasure-arousal diagonals. Pleasure and arousal intensity values were extracted from the scored intensities for these items and were
used to map the average locations in the pleasure-arousal domain at which the different scenes were rated, with and without chair influence.

Fig. 2 shows how the various scenes were rated in terms of pleasure and
arousal, with a distinction between scenes seen with and without chair influence.
Scenes 1 and 2 were chosen to represent quadrant 1 (top right), scenes 3 and 4
quadrant 2 (top left), scenes 5 and 6 quadrant 3 (bottom left) and scenes 7 and 8
quadrant 4 (bottom right). The graph shows the difference in reported pleasure and
arousal intensity between scene presentation with and without chair influence, as
.well as between the different scenes.

A Bonferroni adjusted pairwise comparison of the difference in effect of
the four pleasure-arousal quadrants on pleasure and arousal intensity showed that
the effect on reported intensity of pleasure is not significant between pleasure-
arousal quadrants 1 and 4 and quadrants 2 and 3, which is to be expected as quadrants 1 and 4 are on the same side of the pleasure axis, as are quadrants 2 and 3.
Concerning the effect of the quadrants on arousal intensity a similar effect was
seen, but between quadrant 1 and quadrant 3. The expected similarity between
quadrants 1 and 2 (positive arousal) and quadrants 3 and 4 (negative arousal) does
not show.

Analyses of the reported emotion intensities have not shown any significant effect of chair influence on experienced intensity when split either by quadrant or scene or in aggregated tests. Some significant values were found when the
separate questionnaire items were considered and analyzed per scene. Table 5
gives an overview of the p values that showed significance.

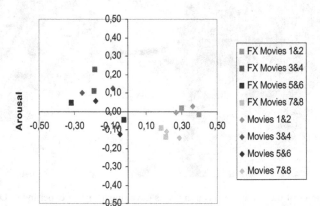

Fig. 2. Average pleasure-arousal mapping of 8 scenes, with and without chair influence (FX).
Similarly colored items represent scenes chosen to fit the same pleasure-arousal quadrant.

Table 5. Overview of p values < 0,05 for the effect of chair influence on the reported intensity for ten questionnaire items, split per scene

Question	Scene	p value
Slow-fast heartbeat	4	0,029
Contentedness-frustration	6	0,038*
Distraction-immersion	5	0,038
Boredom-fascination	1	0,034*
	2	0,03
Unpleasantness-pleasantness	6	0,038*

* Mann-Whitney 2-tailed test did not show significance

Discussion

Considering the data presented in Table 5 we can conclude that this experiment did not succeed in confirming the hypothesis that an emotionally charged multi-modal experience is subjectively experienced as being more intense when the physical states related to those emotions are induced than when this is not the case. Although in some cases intensities significantly differ with influence, there does not seem to be a clear effect. Only scene 1 and 2, which represent the same pleasure-arousal quadrant, show a significant effect on fascination. One might conclude from this that bodily influence did have some effect on scenes high in both pleasure and arousal, but when we look at Fig. 3 we can see that the effect on pleasure is opposite in both scenes, eliminating the possibility to draw such a conclusion.

Fig. 3 and 4 also show the division into pleasure-arousal quadrants of the scenes based on participants' ratings. It seems that in general scenes were rated as being in the quadrant they were selected to represent, with some ambiguity in scenes 5 and 6, which corresponds with the scattering of the items for quadrant 3 seen in Fig. 2.

The design of the experiment described here has led to some choices that

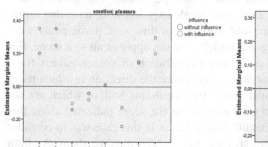
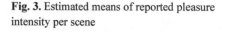
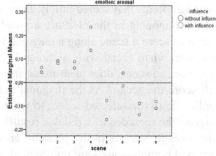

Fig. 3. Estimated means of reported pleasure intensity per scene

Fig. 4. Estimated means of reported arousal intensity per scene

were based on intuition. When scenes were selected to represent each pleasure-arousal quadrant the aim was to find scenes that were pure in the emotional charge they contained and they were selected intuitively (by two independent researchers) to fall into a certain quadrant of Russell's [34] pleasure-activation model. It is therefore interesting to see that at least to some extent this intuitive mapping corresponded with the emotional rating participants gave to the different scenes, even if not all scenes were equally representative of their quadrant. The data leads one to believe that translation of scenes to pleasure and arousal components is possible to a certain extent. Even if the current research does not show a great effect of bodily influence on emotion, at least this finding is of interest and of possible use in further research.

Another problem was the subtlety of influence, or lack thereof. Technical imperfections in the chair hindered implicit bodily influence and made the user more aware of the fact that they were being influenced than should have been the case. Speed of posture change was too high, and there was more than one source of noise when the various modalities were activated, confusing and even annoying the participants. Although it produced noise and could be clearly felt throughout the chair, heart rate feedback was not noticed as such by most participants, and there was no significant effect on reported heart rate. Whether this was due to the interruption of the experience or if this modality is simply unable to produce the desired effect remains unclear and may be subject for further research.

Finally, a choice in the presentation of the questionnaire led to a possible problem. Instead of asking participants to recall their experienced emotions for all scenes at the end of the experiment, a choice was made to pause between scenes and have them fill out the questionnaire regarding the last viewed scene to prevent difficulties presented by the recollection of emotions. The result was that participants were not only made aware of their bodily state as such, but even of their emotions as the final question was always to describe the emotions they experienced. Even though hardly any of the participants claimed to know the goal of the experiment at the debriefing, some could guess and it is possible that the implicitness of the emotional influence was endangered simply by making users aware of their emotions and their role in the experiment.

Regarding the analysis of the data, a problem was encountered when deriving the pleasure and arousal intensities scored per scene. The questionnaire contained items that scored purely along one single axis, but also items that represented diagonals in the pleasure-arousal domain. In this way, participants were forced to score a scene along a diagonal which may not apply at all to a scene. For example, when faced with a choice between frustration or contentedness for a happy or sad scene, does pleasure or arousal influence the direction in which users will score the scene? As the diagonal enters two quadrants both of which are not applicable to the selected scene, to what extent can the score indicated along this diagonal be regarded as a reliable result? The solution in this case was to consider all scores as vectors in the pleasure-arousal domain and average them. As both axes and both diagonals are represented, the average vector should still occupy the correct quadrant. Still, the effect of using these diagonals is not quite clear and should perhaps be avoided in future research in order to get a clearer image of how participants experience a movie scene.

This experiment encountered several problems that may have influenced the outcome. These problems consisted mainly of technical issues that hindered the immersion of the participants' experience. On top of that, many will agree that it is difficult to gather unambiguous empirical data when working with people and subjectively experienced emotions.

In conclusion we can say that, in spite of the problems encountered, the fact that movie scenes can be considered in terms of pleasure and arousal is in itself interesting. The main hypothesis of this research is not supported by these results though, but by no means does this indicate that it is not *possible* to enhance an immersive experience through induction of bodily states specific to certain emotional states.

Future Work

More research can provide us with more insight into the possibilities of applying William James' theory of emotion in the entertainment industry.

Some changes should be made to this experiment setup to ensure more reliable and possibly useful data. Such changes would include (1) the use of many more participants, (2) fewer scenes, perhaps only one per quadrant or two per axis, and fewer scenes per subject, (3) blind rating of the emotional charge of selected scenes by a group of independent reviewers prior to experimentation, (4) fewer and clearer questionnaire items in terms of their meaning in pleasure-arousal terms, (5) more subtle influence in terms of noise and speed of position changes.

Regarding the various modalities, some considerations as to the exact implementation should be made as well. In this experiment the chair was fitted with air ventilation to lower the temperature because, among other reasons, it was the quickest and cheapest solution to create. Some people did notice the air flow however and of course the noise from a slow moving fan is an issue. Perhaps a cooling system integrated in the back and seat of the chair would be more functional. Peltier elements may be used for heating as well as cooling if budget allows. In terms of position adjustment, a speed-adjustable, programmable motor with Hall-sensor for position feedback would be the wise choice. As for heart rate feedback, perhaps smaller, silent vibrating elements can be used in the back and seat, although one single vibrating motor on the back was enough to feel a vibration through the entire chair. A silent version of this solution would work well. Finally, other modalities as described earlier can be added as well, although for the purposes of clear and unambiguous results we would advise against an abundance of modalities. Perhaps the various modalities should even be tested separately, in separate experiments, to determine their effectiveness in this field.

Acknowledgements

The authors wish to thank Rob Overkamp and Daniel Attevelt for extensive technical support, Arjen van der Meulen for providing and aiding in the selection of video material and Sofie Brandsteder for her great help with statistical analysis.

References

1. W. James, What is an emotion?, *Mind*, Vol. 9 (1884), pp. 188-205.

2. P. Philippot, G. Chapelle, S. Blairy, Respiratory feedback in the generation of emotion, *Cognition and Emotion*, Vol. 16 (2002) No. 5, pp. 605-627

3. S.E. Duclos, J.D. Laird, E. Schneider, M. Sexter, L. Stern, O. Van Lighten, Emotion-specific effects of facial expressions and postures on emotional experience, *Journal of Personality and Social Psychology*, Vol. 57 (1989) No. 1, pp. 100-108

4. D.N. McIntosh, R.B. Zajonc, P.S. Vig, S.W. Emerick, Facial Movement, Breathing, Temperature and Affect: Implications of the Vascular Theory of Emotional Efference, *Cognition and Emotion*, Vol. 11 (1997) No. 2, pp. 171-195

5. J.H. Riskind, C.C. Gotay, Physical Posture: Could It Have Regulatory or Feedback Effects on Motivation and Emotion?, *Motivation and Emotion*, Vol. 6 (1982) No. 3, pp. 273-298

6. F.A. Boiten, N.H. Frijda, C.J.E. Wientjes, Emotions and respiratory patterns: review and critical analysis, *International Journal of Psychophysiology*, Vol. 17 (1994), pp. 103-128

7. B. Mittelmann, H.G. Wolff, Affective States and Skin Temperature: Experimental Study of Subjects With "Cold Hands" and Raynaud's Syndrome, *Psychosomatic Medicine*, Vol. 1 (1939) No. 2, pp. 271-292

8. E. Briese, Emotional Hyperthermia and Performance in Humans, *Physiology & Behavior*, Vol. 58 (1995) No. 3, pp. 615-618

9. R.A. McFarland, Relationship of Skin Temperature Changes to the Emotions Accompanying Music, *Biofeedback and Self-Regulation*, Vol. 10 (1985) No. 3, pp. 255-267

10. C.A. Anderson, Temperature and Aggression: Ubiquitous Effects of Heat on Occurrence of Human Violence, *Psychological Bulletin*, Vol. 106 (1989) No. 1, pp. 74-96

11. C.A. Anderson, K.B. Anderson, W.E. Deuser, Examining an Affective Aggression Framework: Weapon and Temperature Effects on Aggressive Thoughts, Affect and Attitudes, *Personality and Social Psychology Bulletin*, Vol. 22 (1996) No. 4, pp. 366-376

12. H.Z. Tan, A. Pentland, Tactual Displays for Wearable Computing, *Personal Technologies*, Vol. 1 (1997), pp. 225-230

13. S. Brave, A. Dahley, inTouch: A Medium for Haptic Interpersonal Communication, *CHI 97*, (1997) 22-27 March, pp. 363-364

14. D. Mathew, vSmileys: Imaging Emotions through Vibration Patterns, *Alternative Access: Feelings and Games 2005*, (2005) Spring

15. A.F. Rovers, H.A. Van Essen, HIM: A Framework for Haptic Instant Messaging, *CHI 2004*, (2004) April 24-29, pp. 1313-1316

16. S. Yohanan, M. Chan, J. Hopkins, H. Sun, K. MacLean, Hapticat: Exploration of Affective Touch, *ICMI'05*, (2005) October 4-6, pp. 222-22

17. M.D.Decaria, S. Proctor, T.E. Malloy, The effect of false heart rate feedback on self-reports of anxiety and on actual heart rate, *Behavior Research & Therapy*, Vol. 12 (1974), pp. 251-253

18. K.T. Larkin, S.B. Manuck, A.L. Kasprowicz, The Effect of Feedback-Assisted Reduction in Heart Rate Reactivity on Videogame Performance, *Biofeedback and self-regulation*, Vol. 15 (1990) No. 4, pp. 285-303

19. E.H. Liebhart, Effects of False Heart Rate Feedback and Task Instructions on Information Search, Attributions, and Stimulus Ratings, *Psychological Research*, Vol. 39 (1977), pp. 185-202

20. B. Parkinson, L. Colgan, False Autonomic Feedback: Effects of Attention to Feedback on Ratings of Pleasant and Unpleasant Target Stimuli, *Motivation and Emotion*, Vol. 12 (1988) No.1, pp. 87-98

21. C. Collett, E. Vernet-Maury, G. Delhomme, A. Dittmar, Autonomic nervous system response patterns specificity to basic emotions, *Journal of the Autonomic Nervous System*, Vol. 62 (1997), pp. 45-57

22. H.D. Critchley, R. Elliott, C.J. Mathias, R.J. Dolan, Neural Activity Relating to Generation and Representation of Galvanic Skin Conductance Responses: A Functional Magnetic Resonance Imaging Study, *The Journal of Neuroscience*, Vol. 20 (2000) No. 8, pp. 3033-3040

23. H.D. Critchley, Electrodermal Responses: What Happens in the Brain, *Neuroscientist*, Vol. 8 (2002) No. 2, pp. 132-142

24. W. Hubert, R. De Jong-Meyer, Psychophysiological Response Patterns to Positive and Negative Film Stimuli, *Biological Psychology*, Vol. 31 (1990), pp. 73-93

25. S. Khalfa, P. Isabelle, B. Jean-Pierre, R. Manon, Event-related skin conductance responses to musical emotions in humans, *Neuroscience Letters*, Vol. 328 (2002), pp. 145-149

26. A. Pecchinenda, C.A. Smith, The Affective Significance of Skin Conductance Activity During a Difficult Problem-Solving Task, *Cognition and Emotion*, Vol. 10 (1996) No. 5, pp. 481-503

27. A.J. Ferreira, W.D. Winter, The Palmar Sweat Print: A Methodological Study, *Psychosomatic Medicine*, Vol. 22 (1963) No. 4, pp. 377-384

28. B. Mittelmann, H.G. Wollf, Affective States and Skin Temperature: Experimental Study of Subjects With "Cold Hands" and Raynaud's Syndrome, *Psychosomatic Medicine*, Vol. 1 (1939) No. 2, pp. 271-292

29. J.A. Allen, J.E. Armstrong, I.C. Roddie, The Regional Distribution of Emotional Sweating in Man. *Journal of Physiology*, Vol. 235 (1973) No. 3, pp. 749-759

30. G. Epple, R.S. Herz, Ambient Odors Associated to Failure Influence Cognitive Performance in Children, *Developmental Psychobiology*, Vol. 35 (1999), pp. 103-107

31. R.S. Herz, J. Eliassen, S. Beland, T. Souza, Neuroimaging evidence for the emotional potency of odor-evoked memory, *Neuropsychologia*, Vol. 42 (2004), pp. 371-378

32. A.N. Rétiveau, E. Chambers IV, G.A. Milliken, Common and Specific Effects of Fine Fragrances on the Mood of Women, *Journal of Sensory Studies*, Vol. 19 (2004), pp. 373-394

33. J. Haviland-Jones, D.J. McGuire, The Scents of Fear and Funny, *The Aroma-Chology Review*, Vol. 8 (1999) No. 2, pp. 11

34. J.A. Russell, Core Affect and the Psychological Construction of Emotion, *Psychological Review*, Vol. 110 (2003) No. 1, pp. 145-172

Networked Virtual Marionette Theater

Daisuke Ninomiya[1], Kohji Miyazaki[1], Ryohei Nakatsu[1,2]

1 Kwansei Gakuin University, School of Science and Technology
2-1 Gakuen, Sanda, 669-1337 Japan
{aaz61232, miyazaki, nakatsu}@kwansei.ac.jp
http:www.kwansei.ac.jp

[2]National University of Singapore, Interactive & Digital Media Institure
Block E3A, #02-04, 7 Engineering Drive 1, Singapore 117574
idmdir@nus.edu.sg
http://www.idmi.nus.edu.sg

Abstract. This paper describes a system that allows users to control virtual marionette characters based on computer graphics (CG marionette characters) with their
hand and finger movements and thus perform a marionette theatrical play. The
system consists of several subsystems, and each subsystem consists of a web camera and a PC. It can recognize a hand gesture of its user and transform it into a
gesture of a CG marionette character. These subsystems are connected through the
Internet, so they can exchange the information of the CG marionette character's
movements at each subsystem and display the movements of all characters
throughout the entire system. Accordingly, multiple users can join the networked
virtual marionette theater and enjoy the marionette play together.

Keywords: Marionette, puppet, virtual theater, hand gesture, image recognition

1 Introduction

The culture of controlling puppets with the hands to perform theatrical play has
been common throughout the world from ancient times. In Japan, there is a type of
puppet theater called Bunraku, which arose about three hundred years ago [1][2].
In Europe, too, various kinds of puppet play have been performed and enjoyed.
The puppet play using a puppet called a "marionette" has been the most popular
variety [3]. Marionette play and puppets have become very popular in recent
years, largely due to the movie called "Strings [4]" (Fig. 1). This paper describes a

Please use the following format when citing this chapter:

Ninomiya, D., Miyazaki, K. and Nakatsu, R., 2008, in IFIP International Federation for Information Processing, Volume 279; *New Frontiers for Entertainment Computing*; Paolo Ciancarini, Ryohei Nakatsu, Matthias Rauterberg, Marco Roccetti; (Boston: Springer), pp. 49–58.

networked virtual marionette theater that is basically a distributed system consisting of several subsystems connected through the Internet. Each subsystem can recognize the hand and finger gestures of the person in front of its web camera and then transform them into the motions of a marionette character based on computer graphics (CG marionettes). Each subsystem exchanges the information of actions performed by its marionette character with such information from the other subsystems. The display of each subsystem shows a virtual scene where multiple marionette characters, each controlled by a different user, interact. Thus multiple users, even if they are in separate locations, can gather in a virtual marionette theater and perform a theatrical marionette play.

Fig. 1. A scene of "Strings"

2 Related Works

Technologies based on three-dimensional computer graphics have made tremendous progress in recent years. We can see photographically real CG objects and CG characters in movies and games. Furthermore, the technologies based on CG animation have also progressed rapidly. Animations of fluid [5] and the destruction of objects [6] have been studied. Moreover, the movements of a crowd based on an artificial-intelligence approach [7] and movements of humans based on inverse kinematics [8] have been proposed. Motion capture systems have been widely used for the control of CG characters [9]. Although the realization of human-like motions of CG characters has been eagerly pursued, the realization of marionette-like motions has seldom been studied. Since the movements of marionette characters are unique and have been loved by people throughout history, it is worth studying a system by which non-experts of marionettes can easily manipulate their movements and generate marionette-like behaviors using CG characters.

3 System Concept

The following elements typically compose a marionette theater.
(1) Puppets called "marionettes"
(2) Speech of each puppet
(3) Scene settings
(4) Music

In a large performance, various kinds of marionette puppets appear and the scene settings are changed frequently, depending on the story's plot, and even a live orchestra is sometimes used to generate music. Therefore, even if people wanted to enjoy manipulating marionette puppets and creating theatrical play, it could be very difficult. On the other hand, if we introduced virtual marionette characters based on computer graphics instead of using real marionettes with physical bodies, it would become significantly easier for users to generate and change most of the above elements of marionettes, speech, backgrounds, and music. In addition, by developing a networked virtual marionette theater, multiple users, manipulating their own marionette characters, can gather in a virtual theater and let their virtual puppets interact with other puppets, thus creating the performance of a virtual theatrical play.

4 System Structure

4.1 Overview

The entire system is made from a group of subsystems connected through a network. The structure of the whole system is shown in Fig. 2, and the structure of each subsystem is illustrated in Fig. 3. Each subsystem consists of a PC and a web camera. The posture of a user's hand is captured by the web camera, and then hand-gesture recognition is carried out. Then the recognition result of a hand posture is reflected in the gestures of a CG marionette character.

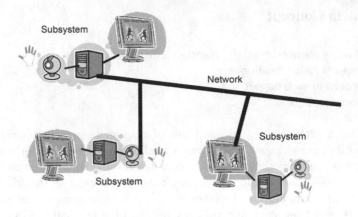

Fig. 2. Structure of entire system

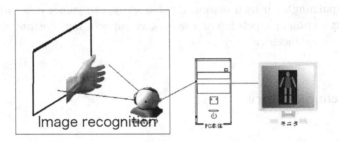

Fig. 3. Structure of subsystem

4.2 *Hand-gesture recognition*

In this section, a real-time hand-gesture recognition method is described for use in the recognition of a user's hand gesture for each subsystem [5]. There have been several research efforts on the real-time recognition of hand gestures [6][7]. Most of them use rather complicated systems such as multiple cameras. On the other hand, we tried to develop a simpler system using a single web camera. The recognition process consists of the following sub-processes.

4.2.1 Extraction of hand area (Fig. 4)

Using the color information of a hand, the image area corresponding to a hand is extracted from the background. In this case, HSV information obtained by the transformation of RGB information is used. Then, using a median filter, the noise contained in the extracted image is deleted.

Fig. 4. Extraction of hand area

4.2.3 Extraction of finger information using histogram

The length of each finger is calculated by using simple histogram information. Figure 5 shows the information of a histogram corresponding to finger length. Depending on the angle of finger bending, the height of the histogram varies. This means that from the height information of the histogram, the bending angle of a finger can be calculated.

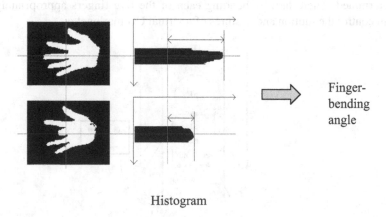

Finger-bending angle

Histogram

Fig. 5. Extraction of finger-length information

4.2.4 Optimization of separating each finger's histogram

Depending on the angle of each finger against the x axis (or y axis), it is some-times difficult to clearly separate a histogram corresponding to each finger. There-fore, for the information extraction of each finger, rotation transformation is car-ried out to achieve the optimum separation of partial histograms corresponding to each finger.

4.2.5 Bending-angle estimation of each finger

Figure 5 also shows a comparison between two histograms varying with the bending angle of a finger. By comparing the length of a histogram to the original (longest) histogram when the bending angle is zero, the bending angle of the fin-ger is calculated.

4.3 Control of CG marionette

Each finger is assumed connected to a certain part of a CG marionette through a virtual string. The relationship between five strings and the part of the marionette to which each string is attached is illustrated in Fig. 6. Here, t1 ~ t5 are virtual stings, and p1 ~ p8 are the parts composing the marionette model, where a1 ~ a7 are joints of these parts. The bending angle of each finger calculated in the above process is reflected directly in the length of each string. In this way, the angle of each joint of the marionette, corresponding to p1, p2, p3, p4, p5, p6, p7, and p8, is determined. Therefore, by bending each of the five fingers appropriately, a user can control the motion and gestures of a virtual CG marionette.

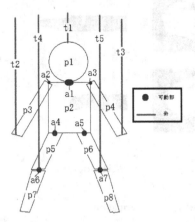

Fig. 6. Model of a virtual marionette

4.4 Background and CG characters

We are planning a system that allows us to easily change scenes as well as characters, so we have developed various kinds of backgrounds and characters based on computer graphics. We are trying to develop an "Interactive Folktale System [8]" that offer users the ability to generate Japanese folktales as animation and to enjoy the interactions with creators of other characters in the system. Therefore, we have prepared various kinds of backgrounds and characters for our virtual marionette system. Figure 7 shows one of the marionette character in three different backgrounds.

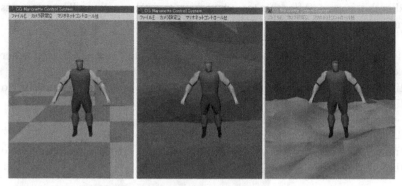

Fig. 7. Examples of virtual marionette characters

4.5 Networked marionette theater

The virtual marionette system we have developed as a first prototype toward the networked virtual marionette system consists of a hand-gesture recognition unit and an animation generation unit. This prototype system would work as a subsystem in the distributed system. In each subsystem, the recognition results of the other subsystems are shared. Furthermore, all of the CG characters and backgrounds are shared among these subunits. Using these recognition results as well as the CG characters and backgrounds, each subsystem can simultaneously create the same scene where multiple CG characters, each of which is controlled by its own subsystem, appear and behave in the same way.

5   Evaluation of the System

We have carried out an evaluation of a subsystem, which is the basis of the whole system and the instrument with which a user can control one virtual marionette character. We selected 20 students as subjects for this evaluation's tests. All of them know about marionette puppets but have never manipulated them. We asked them to manipulate both a real marionette puppet and a virtual CG marionette used in this system. After that we asked them several questions. The questions and the answers are summarized as follows.

(1) Is the movement of a virtual marionette "unique" compared with other CG characters?
Definitely Yes (4), Comparatively Yes (12), Neutral (4), Comparatively No (0), Definitely No (0)

(2) Is the movement of a virtual marionette "real"?
Definitely Yes (0), Comparatively Yes (1), Neutral (15), Comparatively No (4), Definitely No (0)

(3) Did you feel that your hand gestures were closely reflected in the movements of a virtual marionette?
Definitely Yes (0), Comparatively Yes (15), Neutral (3), Comparatively No (1), Definitely No (1)

From the first question, it is clear that 80% of the subjects said that there is some unique aspect in the movement of the virtual marionette. This means that the authors succeeded in their intention to develop a system in which the particular movement of a marionette is regenerated. For the second question, the fact that most of the subjects answered "neutral" indicates that the meaning of "real" is somewhat difficult for them to associate with the marionette's movement. For the third question, 75% of the subjects answered that the marionette correctly moved according to their hand gestures. These results show that the recognition method introduced here works very well and gives people the feeling that they are directly manipulating the virtual marionette characters. Moreover, they again expressed the feeling that the system successfully reproduced the particular movement of a marionette.

6 Conclusions

In this paper, we proposed a system in which users can easily manipulate virtual marionette characters with their hand gestures. For the recognition of hand gestures, simple real-time hand-gesture recognition was realized by using histogram information of an extracted hand area. The recognition result is reflected in the movement of the marionette character by connecting each finger movement to a particular part of the virtual marionette by a virtual string. Furthermore, the concept of networked marionette theater was proposed in which several subsystems are connected by a network. Here, multiple users can perform theatrical marionette play by manipulating their own marionette characters. Finally, we carried out an evaluation test to assess the feasibility of a subsystem. By using twenty subjects and letting them manipulate both a physical marionette as well as a virtual one, we obtained evaluation results indicating that by using this virtual marionette system, even a non-expert of marionette manipulation can have the feeling of manipulating marionettes and thus can participate in a theatrical marionette performance.

For our further work, we need to improve the recognition accuracy of the hand-gesture recognition. Moreover, we need to develop adequate contents to refine the entire networked virtual marionette theater, and we also need to carry out an evaluation of the whole system by letting people use the system.

References

1. Keene, D. *No and Bunraku.* (1990). Columbia University Press.
2. http://www.lares.dti.ne.jp/bunraku/index.html
3. Currell D. *Making and Manipulating Marionettes.* (2004). The Crowood Press Ltd.
4. http://www.futuremovies.co.uk/review.asp?ID=319
5. Stam, J. and Fiume, E. Depicting Fire and Other Gaseous Phenomena Using Diffusion Process. (1995). *In Proceedings of SIGGRAPH'95.*
6. O' Brien, J. F. and Hodgins J. K. Graphical modeling and animation of brittle fracture. (1999). *In Proceedings of SIGGRAPH'99.*
7. Courty, N. Fast Crowd. (2004). *In Proceedings of SIGGRAPH ' 2004.*
8. Boulic N., Thalmann, M. and Thalmann, D. A GLOBAL HUMAN WALKING MODEL WITH REAL-TIME KINEMATIC PERSONIFICATION. (1990). *The Visual computer*, pp. 344-358.
9. Lee, J. and Lee, K. H. Precomputing avatar behavior from human motion data. (2004). *Graphical Models*, Vol. 68, No. 2, pp. 158-174.
10. Ninomiya, D., Miyazaki, K. and Nakatsu, R. Study on the CG Marionette Control Based on the Hand Gesture Recognition. (2006). *Annual Meeting of Game Society of Japan* (in Japanese).
11. Ng, C. W. Real-time gesture recognition system and application. (2002). *Image and Vision Computing*, pp. 20.

12. Utsumi, A., Ohya, J. and Nakatsu, R. Multiple-camera-based Multiple-hand-gesture-tracking. (1999). *Transaction of Information Processing Society of Japan*, Vol. 40, No. 8, pp. 3143-3154 (in Japanese).
13. Miyazaki, K., Nagai, Y., Wama, T. and Nakatsu, R. Concept and Construction of an Interactive Folktale System. (2007). *Entertainment Computing – ICEC2007*, Springer LNCS 4740, pp. 162-170.

Entertainment Computing in the Orbit

Matthias Rauterberg[1], Mark Neerincx[2], Karl Tuyls[1], Jack van Loon[3]

[1] Eindhoven University of Technology, The Netherlands
[2] TNO Human Factors & TU Delft, The Netherlands
[3] DESC Space Flight/Microgravity & ACTA Free University Amsterdam, The Netherlands
g.w.m.rauterberg@tue.nl, mark.neerincx@tno.nl, j.vanloon@vumc.nl

Abstract: During ultra long space missions (i.e. to Mars), the isolated space environment affects a number of physiological, psychosocial and mental processes critically involved in human performance, and it is vital to missions' success to understand the psychological limits. Past experiences in space have shown that the mental health of a crew can have a great effect on the success or failure of a mission. Latent and overt stress factors are mental strain, interpersonal problems, and lack of capability to rescue crew members, isolation, monotony, and tedium of life aboard an autonomous shuttle. Abstract These issues develop very slowly over time and are very difficult to detect and remedy for observers on the ground. E.g. long-term isolation can lead to sleep deprivation, depression, irritability, anxiety, impaired cognition, and even hostility. Providing astronauts with entertainment products can help to maintain the mental health of the crew. The results of this project will deepen the understanding of intra- and inter-individual crew behaviour and related performance, and provide the technical platform for a new type of crew assistance tools based on multi-user computer games.
Keywords: astronaut, space research, entertainment, game, mental health.

1 Introduction

The European Space Agency (ESA) has started to roadmap the necessary research for making a manned mission to Mars feasible (see Fig. 1). In 2005 the TU Eindhoven was contacted by the Dutch Experiment Support Center (DESC) to start collaboration on research in entertainment and mental health of a crew on ultra-long space flights (e.g. to Mars). As one of the outcomes of this discussion was setting-up the Dutch Entertainment Computing Consortium (DECC)[1]. In 2006

---

[1] See http://www.org.id.tue.nl/DECC/

Please use the following format when citing this chapter:

Rauterberg, M., et al., 2008, in IFIP International Federation for Information Processing, Volume 279; *New Frontiers for Entertainment Computing*; Paolo Ciancarini, Ryohei Nakatsu, Matthias Rauterberg, Marco Roccetti; (Boston: Springer); pp. 59–70.

DECC organized a workshop at the Lorentz Center (Leiden, The Netherlands)[2] to establish discussions among Dutch researchers in the field of entertainment and health, training and serious gaming. This research project brought together the available state of the art expertise in the Netherlands on man-machine interaction and entertainment, human factors and cognitive task load, evolutionary game theory and multi-agent systems, and Actor-Agent Community technology at DECIS Lab (Delft).

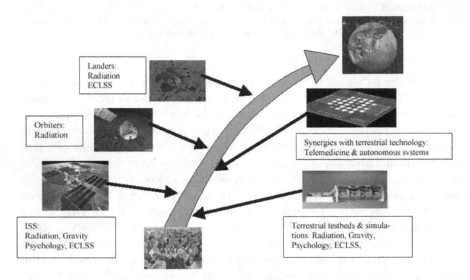

Fig 1: Roadmap with regard to human health issues for a future European strategy towards human exploratory missions.

2 State of the art

The success of human space missions depends among others on the following two factors: (1) each astronaut remains alert and vigilant while operating sophisticated equipment and following complex procedures, and (2) the whole crew can operate and collaborate autonomously and successfully to recover from critical situations. Ultra-long space missions are characterized on the one hand by new physical parameters, on the other hand by new psychosocial parameters. New physical parameters are weightlessness, three-dimensional configuration, and reduced living

---

[2] See http://www.lorentzcenter.nl/lc/web/2006/214/info.php3?wsid=214

space. New psychosocial parameters are small group living, working together in close proximity, and extreme social isolation (Manzey, 2004). Adaptation to this new environment involves a number of mental processes, which includes simultaneously physiological, psychosocial and behavioural modifications in the course of time (Christensen and Talbot, 1986; Tafforin, 1996; Palinkas, 2001; Sandal, 2001a; Manzey, 2004). It is reported that the Russian scientists have taken definitely more interest in studying psychosocial factors affecting their cosmonauts than the American (Kanas, 1985, 1987; Santy, 1983). In spite of a very careful selection and preparation of the crew members, including a test of "psychological compatibility", within a long-term mission already after 30 days the crew began to show signs of hostility (Kanas, 1987).

The space environment in ultra-long missions affects a number of physiological systems critically involved in human performance, and it is vital to mission success to understand the biological, physiological and psychological limits of human performance under such conditions (Palinkas, 2001). It has been demonstrated that both acute gravitational changes and isolation in ultra-long space flight (e.g., social monotony) can lead to stress and performance problems (Endler, 2004). Since e.g. isolation and hyper-arousal result in both psychosocial and performance deficits, this project is focused on (1) a diagnostic tool to measure psychosocial crew health status, and (2) countermeasures to assist crew members improving team communication and collaboration (i.e. [semi] Autonomous Mental Health Assistance, AMHA; see also Rauterberg, 2004). In particular, this project is concerned with the following aspects: altered work-leisure time cycles with related mood problems, and altered or reduced communication and collaboration opportunities among crew members with related possible inter-individual conflicts.

Risks and Goals:

In the human behaviour and performance discipline area the following three risks have been identified as unacceptable risks of serious adverse health and performance consequences without having so far a mitigation strategy that has been demonstrated on Earth or even validated in space (ESTEC 2001; NASA 2004):

- **Risk 1--Area:** Human Behaviour and Performance
  Risk Title: Human performance failure due to poor psychosocial adaptation.
  Risk Description: Human performance failure due to problems associated with adapting interpersonally to the space environment: poor interpersonal relationships and/or group dynamics; and inadequate team cohesiveness.
  Justification: Moderate likelihood/high consequence risk with low mitigation status; need to reduce probability of human error, performance and/or mission failure. Serious interpersonal conflicts have occurred in space flights. The failure of flight crews to cooperate and work effectively with each other or with flight controllers has been a periodic problem in both US and Russian space flight programs. Interpersonal distrust, dislike, misunderstanding and poor communi-

cation have led to potential dangerous situations, such as crew members refusing to speak to one another during critical operations, or withdrawing from voice communication with ground controllers. Such problems of group cohesiveness have a high likelihood of occurrence in ultra-long space flight and if not mitigated through prevention or intervention, they will pose grave risks to the mission.

[*References*: Kanas 1985, 1987; Palinkas 1991, 2001; Suedfeld and Steel 2000; Morphew 2001; Sandal 2001a, 2001b]

Countermeasures: Unobtrusive monitoring and early detection of individual adaptation problems.

- **Risk 2--Area:** Human Behaviour and Performance.
  Risk Title: Human performance failure due to neurobehavioral problems.
  Risk Description: Human performance failure during missions due to such conditions as depression, anxiety, trauma, or other neuro-psychiatric and cognitive problems.
  Justification: Although infrequent, serious neurobehavioral problems involving stress and depression have occurred in space flight, especially during long-duration missions. In some of these instances, the distress has contributed to performance errors during critical operations, such as the collision of Progress into Mir during manual docking. In other instances, emotional problems led to changes in motivation, diet, sleep, and exercise. No matter how carefully selected and prepared crews are for long-duration flights, the US and Russian experiences reveal that at least some subset of astronauts will experience problems with their behavioural health. Long-duration flights will have a significant likelihood of psychiatric problems emerging.
  [*References*: Santy 1987; Kanas 1998; Driskell et al. 1999; Ellis 2000; Palinkas and Houseal 2000; Suedfeld and Steel 2000; Lane and Feeback 2002; Woolford et al. 2002; Kanas 2004; Palinkas et al. 2004]
  Countermeasures: On-board unobtrusive technologies as astronaut's aids for valid detection of stress reactions and cognitive or emotional problems; on-board information technologies as astronauts' aids for management of stress reactions and cognitive or emotional problems; self monitoring of mood; improved diagnostic cognitive self-assessment; improved ability to safely and effectively manage an uncooperative crewmember during mission.

- **Risk 3--Area**: Space Human Factors Engineering.
  Risk Title: Mismatch between crew cognitive capabilities and task demands.
  Risk Description: Human performance failure due to inadequate accommodation of human cognitive limitations and capabilities. If human cognitive performance capabilities are surpassed due to inadequate design of tools, interfaces, tasks or information support systems, mission failure or decreased effectiveness or efficiency may result. Identifying, locating, processing, or evaluating information to make decisions and perform critical tasks in short time-frames in nominal and emergency situations, with limited crew size, relying on strictly lo-

cal resources is extremely subject to human errors.

Justification: Crew members require refresher training and information support systems for numerous tasks during six or more month missions. Psychological literature documents increases in error with time since learning and decreases in error with correctly practicing task. Failure to correctly follow procedures has lead to fatal accidents in commercial aviation, even with greatly over learned tasks.

[References: Torrance 1954; Tafforin 1996; Ellis 2000; Woolford et al. 2002; Endler 2004]

Countermeasures: Tools for enabling crew autonomy with respect to information retrieval; tools analyzing tasks to identify critical skills and knowledge; tools to enable self-assessment of readiness to perform; onboard training systems that enables successful readiness to perform. Design requirements for communications systems among crewmembers, between crew and mission control, and among crew and intelligent agents that reduce risk of mission failure.

The scope and size of this project does not allow covering the whole area of all three risks, but we propose an innovative countermeasure that addresses several issues in each of these risks. The proposed [semi] AMHA is a desktop virtual reality software that provides a new type of computer mediated communication and collaboration space among crew members, between each crew member and his/her personal buddy/coach in form of a persuasive virtual agent (De Haan et al. 2005). Based on empirical research, diagnostic relevant characteristics of commercially available desktop virtual reality applications will be extracted, and the results will be implemented into the new AMHA. The virtual agent (buddy) will be adaptive in its communication behaviour to serve the following two main purposes: (1) establishing a trustworthy and private relationship to the particular crew member (Neerincx and Streefkerk 2003), and (2) providing an indirect communication channel to other 'buddies' and crew members (Neerincx et al. 2006).

3 Scientific objectives

The scientific objectives are twofold: (1) empirical research investigating communication and collaboration pattern of crews based on *objective behavioural patterns*, and (2) software engineering research designing and implementing a new type of crew assistance tool using *agent technology*. The outcome of the empirical research will be used as input for the technical specifications and later for validation of the prototype.

Goal 1: Reduce the risk of human physiological or psychosocial performance failure by investigating countermeasures based on adaptive single- and multi-user game/agent technology for unobtrusive onboard training, counseling and diagnostic of individual and crew behavior.

Goal 2: Develop new methods and tools for unobtrusive monitoring of actual mental and social status of crew cooperation and individual performance guaranteeing the privacy of crew members.

Goal 3: Develop Earth-based applications of adaptive multi-user game/agent technologies for diagnosing, assessing, and training crew members to reduce the risk of mental and psychosocial performance failure.

In the next section we describe the technical objectives to realize the AMHA. The final result will be a running prototype to demonstrate and validate relevant concepts and functionality, and to investigate and assess the *potential* of our proposed approach for future research in this direction.

3.1 Research methodology and technical feasibility

This project will executed in three phases: (phase 1) data gathering and analysis in the context of a confinement study with commercial available software (i.e., single and multi user applications) added with automatic user actions logging; (phase 2) developing a software platform to demonstrate the basic concepts of the diagnostic functionality and intended computer mediated communication for the AMHA; and (phase 3) empirical validation of the developed AMHA prototype (cf. Neerincx and Lindenberg 2007). Diagnostic relevant and valid information about the actual relationship among crew members has to satisfy the following requirements: (1) unconstrained behavior for starting and ending collaboration, (2) all crew members should be getting involved, and (3) unobtrusive measuring procedures. Any application that can fulfill these basic requirements seems to be a possible platform. Before we describe each phase in more detail we have to introduce some basic concepts of desktop virtual reality worlds in the context of simulation and gaming, and our conclusions related to this project.

A multiuser online role-playing game (MORPG) is an online computer role-playing game (RPG) in which a number of users interact with one another in a desktop virtual reality world. As in all RPGs, users assume the role of a virtual character and take control over many of that character's actions. MORPGs are distinguished from single-user or small multi-user RPGs by the number of users, and by the game's persistent world, usually hosted by the game's publisher. A persistent world is a desktop virtual reality world that is used as a setting for a role-playing game, often online. The world is always available and world events happen continually. The persistency comes from maintaining and developing the state of the gaming world around the clock. Unlike with other games, a persistent world game's plots and events continue to develop even while some of the users are not playing their character. The comparison is to the real world where events occur that are not directly connected to a user, or continue to happen while a user sleeps, etc. Likewise, a user's character can also influence and change a persistent world. The degree to which a character can affect a world varies from game to game. Persistent worlds do also exist in offline games. Even though technically nothing happens while the game is off, the illusion of persistency is created by advancing events as soon as the game is turned on and using the game engine's clock as a guide for what should have happened, making it seem like events occurred while the game was off. MORPGs are considered by Bonk and Dennen (2005) as serious candidates for assessment and training in the military domain. There are many different user types in a MORPG environment. In a fairly simple taxonomy, Bartle (1996) identified four key roles: achievers, explorers, socializers, and killers. These roles may arise from the interrelationship of two dimensions of playing style: (1) action versus interaction, and (2) world-oriented versus player-oriented. In addition, role assignments have the potential to be an important factor in educational use. For example, it is possible that certain roles foster particular types of learning. Users could be encouraged to assume roles that are most fitting with their task requirements. Alternatively, they might be required to rotate through roles to experience the computer mediated collaboration space from a variety of perspectives.

Conclusion: We propose to build upon such a desktop virtual reality world in form of a MORPG enhanced with virtual agents ('buddies'). Crew members can login at any time to continue their on-going interactions inside this world. In particular they can set up a private relationship with their buddy for communication, and with other crew members for collaborations.

Autonomy is a social notion, and recent research in artificial intelligence has been linked to many social theories. Delegation theory is one such social theory. In many cases the user (or the delegating agent) needs local and decentralized knowledge and decision from the delegated agent (Tuyls and Nowe 2005). This agent-- delegated to take care of a given task-- has to choose from among different possible plans, or to adapt abstract or previous plans to suit new situations; it has to find additional (local and updated) information; it has to solve a problem and not just to execute a function, an action, or implement a recipe; sometimes it has to exploit its 'expertise'. In all these cases this agent takes care of the interests or goals of the former 'remotely', i.e., far from it and without its monitoring and intervention (control), and autonomously. This requires an 'open delegation' (Hexmoor et al. 2008). The virtual agent is supposed to use its knowledge, its intelligence, and its ability, and to exert a degree of discretion.

Conclusion: We propose to design the buddy agent with sufficient autonomy for a set of different tasks (e.g., assessing the mental health status of the related crewmember and providing individual feedback only to protect privacy; communicating with other buddies to assess the entire psychosocial crew status, checking and updating email connection with Earth, etc.).

Social norms are cultural phenomena that naturally emerge in human societies and help prescribe and proscribe normative patterns of behavior. In recent times, the discipline of multi-agent systems has been modeling social norms in artificial society of agents. Hexmoor et al. (2006) reviews norms in multi-agent systems and then offers exploration of a series of norms in a simulation study. Using game theoretic concepts they define and offer an account of norm stability. Particularly in small groups, for the norm of cooperation to evolve and be stable, a relatively small number of individuals with cooperative attitude are needed.

Conclusion: We propose to build in such functionality for the virtual agents to enable social norm stability among crewmembers.

Over the last few years the combination of Evolutionary Game Theory (EGT) and Reinforcement Learning (RL) have proved to be powerful theories for designing autonomous agents, and under-standing interactions in systems composed of such agents (Tuyls et al. 2006). Modeling agents for an assistive tool requires a thorough understanding of the type and form of interactions within the virtual environment and other agents in the tool controlled by users. Instead of assuming that agents are perfectly rational, EGT treats agents' objectives as a matter of fact, with a presumption that these objectives must be compatible with an appropriate evolutionary dynamic (i.e., the replicator dynamics). For this reason, EGT can be used to analyze how agents can make less purely self-interested decisions in complex environments such as adaptive games (Spronk 2005).

Conclusion: Modeling and implementing the virtual agents ('buddy') will be based on EGT and RL.

Conventional media technologies have been designed to primarily handle multimedia, informative, logical communications based on logic and aiming for the user's understanding of a message. This is a narrow view on the communication capabilities of humans and Kansei Mediation offers new opportunities (Nakatsu et al. 2006). It is a style of lifelong learning that possesses a rich combination of communication channels to let direct and indirect information flow freely. Nakatsu et al. (2006) discusses how human–human communication can be delivered indirectly using different modalities. The metaphor of the 'four-ears-model' distinguishes four important dimensions of any human message: (1) content ("what are the facts"), (2) appeal ("what does s/he want me to do, think, feel, etc."), (3) relationship ("what does s/he think about me") and (4) self-disclosure ("what kind of person is s/he"). In communicating the sender sends messages about the subject, which tell something about him/herself about his perception of the relationship with the receiver and which appeal to the receiver to change in some way. One can say the sender talks with four different 'beaks'. To understand the sender well the receiver should listen with four 'ears' and each 'ear' should be tuned to what the corresponding 'beak' tries to say. If the 'beak' and the 'ear' are not in tune with each other, this is one of the main causes for misunderstandings.

Conclusion: We propose to enhance the user interface in addition to visual and audio with haptic feedback.

A first informal user requirement analysis was done with the astronaut Gerhard Thiele (ESA-EAC). He recommends the following requirements: (1) mixed gen-

der crew, (2) strict confidentiality and privacy for the interaction with and through
AMHA, and (3) adaptive tools (e.g., e-learning) to support crew-members
achieving their private learning goals throughout a mission.

Conclusion: We will design the interaction with AMHA so that adaptation and
privacy is guaranteed.

Due to the microgravity constrains under real ultra long flight conditions any
interface concept based on tangible interactions seems to be not appropriate (see
Rauterberg et al., 1997).

3.2 Work plan

For the first phase of this project we plan to get access to a confinement study for
long duration missions (e.g., Mars-500 confinement study, ESA space flights to
ISS) as an empirical test bed. We plan to provide a PC platform with a set of
commercial games: for individual social interaction (e.g., Sims-2), for individual
training (e.g. SpaceStationSim, BioSim), and for inter individual interactions (e.g.,
Age of Empires, Baldur's Gate, XBlast TNT). This PC platform might be extended
with a special logging functionality (e.g. NOLDUS uLog Pro plus Observer XT)
to collect automatically the objective data generated by users during inter-actions.
We will relate the results with additional subjective data gathered by questionnaires and interviews (e.g., a sociogram) to extract diagnostic relevant information
out of the logged data stream (Rauterberg 2003). All necessary facilities [e.g. special analyzing tools like Automatic Mental Model Evaluator, AMME (Rauterberg
1993)] are available within our laboratories.

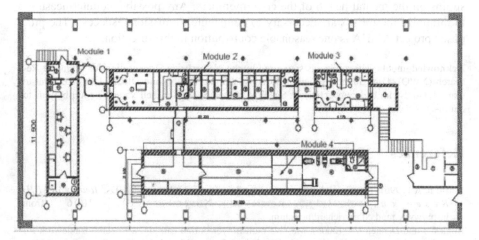

Fig 2: Layout of the mock space station: module 1=medical module, module 2=living
quarters, module 3=Mars landing module, module 4=storage module[3]

---

[3] Taken from
http://spaceflight.esa.int/users/downloads/ao2007/Mars500%20Call%20for%20Candidates.pdf

4 The Mars-500 confinement study

European and Russian space researchers will lock six men in a metal confinement to mimic the stresses and challenges of a manned mission to Mars. First a 100 and later a 500 days experiment, under development by the Russian Institute of Medical and Biological Problems, will put human volunteers in a mock space station module (see Fig. 2) in complete isolation to study how a ultra-long mission to Mars might affect its human crew (Johnson et al. 2003).

During these two studies, the crew will depend on a preset limit of supplies, including about five tons of food and oxygen and three tons of water. A doctor will accompany volunteers inside the module to treat illnesses and injuries. Volunteers will be allowed to quit the experiment only if they develop a severe ailment of psychological stress. During the simulation the crew will watch Earth disappear into the blackness of space as they munch on the same kinds of food available on the International Space Station. ESA will even attempt to simulate the 40-minute time delay for radio signals to travel from the spacecraft to Earth and back, as the crew work and live in extremely isolated conditions.

5 Conclusions

It is obvious that serious research still has to be done to investigate the effects of ultra-long space missions in a confined environment under microgravity constrains on the mental health of the crew members. Any possible countermeasures to minimize these risks are necessary to contribute to missions' success. The proposed project AMHA is one reasonable contribution in this direction.

Acknowledgments. This project is sponsored by the Netherlands Organisation for Scientific Research (NWO), User Support Program Space Research (SRON) and DECIS Lab. We want to thank J. Goldstein, K. Nieuwenhuis, P. Suedfeld and B. Salem for their valuable contributions to our discussions.

References

Bartle R A (1996). Hearts, clubs, diamonds, spades: Players who suit MUDs. *Journal of MUD Research*, vol. 1(1). Retrieved November 10, 2006 from http://www.mud.co.uk/richard/hcds.htm.

Bonk C J and Dennen V P (2005). Massive multiplayer online gaming: a research framework for military training and education. *ADL Technical Report 2005-1*, US State Department of Defense.

Christensen J M and Talbot J M (1986). A review of the psychological aspects of space flight. *Aviation, Space, and Environmental Medicine*, vol. 57(3), pp. 203-212.

De Haan G, van der Mast C A P G, Blanson Henkemans O and Neerincx M A (2005). SuperAssist: Personal assistants for cooperative healthcare treatment. In: M Al-Akaidi and L Rothkrantz (eds.), *Proceedings Euromedia 2005* (pp. 124-128). Toulouse, France: EUROSIS.

Driskell J E, Salas E and Johnston J (1999). Does stress lead to a loss of team perspective? *Group Dynamics: Theory, Research, and Practice*, vol. 3(4), pp. 291-302.

Ellis S R (2000) Collision in space: human factors elements of the Mir Progress 234 collision. *Ergonomics in Design*, pp. 4-9.

Endler N S (2004). The joint effects of person and situation factors on stress in spaceflight. *Aviation, Space, and Environmental Medicine*, vol. 75(7), pp. C22-C27.

ESTEC (2001). HUMEX: Study on the survivability and adaptation of humans to long-duration interplanetary and planetary environments. *HUMEX Technical Note 2* (version 1), ESTEC/Contract No. 14056/99/NL/PA.

Hexmoor H, Castelfranchi C and Falcone R (2008, forthcoming). A prospectus on agent autonomy. In: H Hexmoor and S Brainov (eds.), *Agent Trust* (in planning stage).

Hexmoor H, Venkata S G and Hayes D (2006). Modelling social norms in multiagent systems. *Journal of Experimental and Theoretical Artificial Intelligence*, vol. 18(1), pp. 49-71.

Johnson J C, Boster J S and Palinkas L A (2003). Social roles and the evolution of networks in extreme and isolated environments. *Journal of Mathematical Sociology*, vol. 27, pp. 89-121.

Kanas N (1985). Psychosocial factors affecting simulated and actual space missions. *Aviation, Space, and Environmental Medicine*, vol. 56, pp. 806-811.

Kanas N (1987). Psychological and interpersonal issues in space. *American Journal of Psychiatry*, vol. 144(6), pp. 703-709.

Kanas N (1998). Psychiatric issues affecting long-duration space missions. *Aviation, Space, and Environmental Medicine*, vol. 69, pp. 1211-1216.

Kanas N (2004). Group interactions during Space missions. *Aviation, Space, and Environmental Medicine*, vol. 75(1), pp. C3-C5.

Lane H W and Feeback D L (2002). Habitability and environmental factors: the future of closed-environment tests. In: H W Lane, R L Sauer and D L Feeback (eds.) *ISOLATION: NASA experiments in closed environment living* (pp. 419-432). San Diego, CA: American Astronautical Society.

Manzey D (2004). Human missions to Mars: new psychological challenges and research issues. *Acta Astronautica*, vol. 55, pp. 781-790.

Morphew M E (2001). Psychological and Human Factors in Long Duration Spaceflight. *McGill Journal of Medicine*, vol. 6(1), pp. 74-80.

Nakatsu R, Rauterberg M and Salem B (2006). Forms and theories of communication: From multimedia to Kansei mediation. *Multimedia Systems*, vol. 11(3), pp. 304-312.

NASA (2004). Bioastronautics Critical Path Roadmap (BCPR): an approach to risk reduction and management for human space flight--extending the boundaries. *Document JSC 62577 (draft)*, NASA.

Neerincx M A and Streefkerk J W (2003). Interacting in desktop and mobile context: Emotion, trust and task performance. In: Aarts, E., Collier, R., van Loenen, E. & de Ruyter, B. (Eds.), *Ambient Intelligence: EUSAI 2003*. Lecture Notes in Computer Science (pp. 119-132), Springer.

Neerincx M A, Lindenberg J, Smets N, Grant T, Bos A, Olmedo Soler A,. Brauer U and Wolff M (2006). Cognitive engineering for long duration missions: human-machine collaboration on the Moon and Mars. In: Proceedings of *2nd IEEE International Conference on Space Mission Challenges for Information Technology* (pp. 40-46), Los Alamitos, California: IEEE.

Palinkas L A (1991). Effects of physical and social environments on the health and well-being of Antarctic winter-over personnel. *Environment & Behavior*, vol. 23(6), pp. 782-799.

Palinkas L A (2001). Psychosocial issues in long-term space flights: overview. *Gravitational and Space Biology Bulletin*, vol. 14(2), pp. 25-33.

Palinkas L A and Houseal M (2000). Stages of change in mood and behaviour during a winter in Antarctica. *Environment and Behavior*, vol. 32(1), pp. 128-141.

Palinkas L A, Johnson J C and Boster J S (2004). Social support and depressed mood in isolated and confined environments. *Acta Astronautica*, vol. 54, pp. 639-647.

Rauterberg, M., Bichsel, M., Meier, M., Fjeld, M. (1997). A gesture based interaction technique of a planning tool for construction and design. In: *Proceedings 6th IEEE International Workshop on Robot and Human Communication--RO-MAN'97*, (IEEE Catalog Number: 97TH8299, pp. 212-217). Piscataway: IEEE Press.

Rauterberg M (1993). AMME: an Automatic Mental Model Evaluation to analyze user behaviour traced in a finite, discrete state space. *Ergonomics*, vol. 36(11), pp. 1369-1380.

Rauterberg M (2003). Determinants for collaboration in networked multi-user games. In: R Nakatsu and J Hoshino (eds.), *Entertainment Computing--Technologies and Applications* (pp. 313-321). IFIP, Kluwer Academic Press.

Rauterberg, M. (2004). Positive effects of entertainment technology on human behaviour. In: R. Jacquart (ed.), *Building the Information Society* (pp. 51-58). IFIP, Kluwer Academic Press.

Sandal G M (2001a). Psychosocial issues space: future challenges. *Gravitational and Space Biology Bulletin*, vol. 14(2), pp. 47-54.

Sandal G M (2001b). Crew tension during a space station simulation. *Environment and Behavior*, vol. 33(1), pp. 134-150.

Santy P (1983). The journey out and in: psychiatry and space exploration. *American Journal of Psychiatry*, vol. 140, pp. 519-527.

Santy P (1987). Psychiatric components of a Health Maintenance Facility (HMF) on space station. *Aviation, Space and Environmental Medicine*, vol. 58, pp. 1219-1224.

Spronk P (2005). *Adaptive Game AI*. PhD Thesis, IKAT-University of Maastricht, Netherlands.

Suedfeld P and Steel G D (2000). The environmental psychology of capsule habitants. *Annual Review of Psychology*, vol. 51, pp. 227-253.

Tafforin C (1996). Ethological analysis of crew member behaviour: distance, orientations, and postures. *Advances in Space Biology and Medicine*, vol. 5, pp. 263-281.

Torrance E P (1954). The behaviour of small groups under stress conditions of "survival". *American Sociological Review*, vol. 19(6), pp. 751-755.

Tuyls K and Nowe A (2005). Evolutionary game theory and multi-agent reinforcement learning. *The Knowledge Engineering Review*, vol. 20(1), pp. 63-90.

Tuyls K, 't Hoen P J and Vanschoenwinkel B (2006). An evolutionary dynamical analysis of multi-agent learning in iterated games. *The Journal of Autonomous Agents and Multi-Agent Systems*, vol. 12(1), pp. 115 - 153.

Walther J B (1997). Group and interpersonal effects in international computer-mediated collaboration. *Human Communication Research*, vol. 23(3), pp. 342-369.

Woolford B, Hudy C, Whitmore M, Berman A, Maida J and Pandya A (2002). In Situ training project: LMLSTP phase III report. In: H W Lane, R L Sauer and D L Feeback (eds.), *ISOLATION: NASA experiments in closed environment living* (pp. 407-417). American Astronautical Society.

A Collaborative Science Learning Game Environment for Informal Science Education: *DinoQuest Online*

Walt Scacchi and Robert Nideffer
Game Culture and Technology Laboratory
University of California, Irvine
Irvine, CA 92697
{wscacchi, nideffer}@uci.edu

Joe Adams
Discovery Science Center
Santa Ana, CA
2500 N. Main St. Santa Ana, CA
714-542-2823

Abstract: We describe concepts and results that arose from the development and deployment of a large-scale collaborative game environment called DinoQuest Online. DQO provides an entertaining experience and approach to informal science education. DQO represents a collection of 13 games for helping school-age children to learn about science (or more specifically, life science and dinosaurs). In this paper, we identify and examine different collaborative group forms that emerged to play DQO. Along the way we provided examples of the collaborative groups and game play from DQO.

Introduction

We have developed a large-scale collaborative game environment deployed in a regional science center that joins physical and online activities in the domain of informal science education. The Discovery Science Center (DSC), located in Santa Ana, CA[1], is a regional science center that families and school groups visit in order to experience a diverse variety of interactive science exhibits. These exhibits bring scientific subjects or concepts to life in a hands-on, fun, and entertaining manner. DSC focuses on interactive exhibits as opposed to passive exhibits of scientific artifacts as might be found in a museum that memorializes the history of scientific concepts, scientists, and inventions. DSC is also situated in municipal region, Orange County, CA, whose population spans large concentrations of ethnic immigrants (from Mexico and Latin America, Asia, Middle East, etc.), as well as very affluent to very poor communities. During 2005, more than 275,000 people engaged in DSC visits or outreach activities, while in 2007 more than 425,000 people were engaged, including 150,000 K-12 students of which nearly 90,000 participated in school group visits to DSC. Thus, DSC [2008] exhibits and educational outreach programs are tailored to meet the interests of different communities, age groups, school educators, and other constituencies.

---

[1] See, for example, http://www.answers.com/topic/santa-ana?cat=travel

---

Please use the following format when citing this chapter:

Scacchi, W., Nideffer, R. and Adams, J., 2008, in IFIP International Federation for Information Processing, Volume 279; *New Frontiers for Entertainment Computing*; Paolo Ciancarini, Ryohei Nakatsu, Matthias Rauterberg, Marco Roccetti; (Boston: Springer), pp. 71–82.

In 2004, effort began at DSC to develop a new interactive game-based exhibit that would focus on dinosaurs as the basis for introducing, demonstrating, and engaging visitors with the concepts from life science (e.g., skeletal systems, elements, and function; digestive system; prey-predator relationships). The life science concepts selected for presentation in the exhibit were those that correspond to curricular topics found in K-6 grade science education standards for California, which are nearly identical to the National Science Education Standards[2]. The UCI Game Culture and Technology Laboratory [UCGameLab 2008] was invited to join this project at this time, and project went into design and operational planning in early 2005. This exhibit was designed to enable the development and deployment of both a physical game-based interactive exhibit at the DSC that would be linked and integrated with a Web-based online game environment. The physical exhibit called *DinoQuest* (DQ) (see Figure 1) became operational in mid 2006, while the online game environment called *DinoQuest Online (DQO)*, went into full-scale operation in 2007. Both DQ and DQO were conceived, designed, and deployed as collaborative science learning game (SLG) environments, and can be evaluated as such. The remainder of this paper focuses on examining and explaining DQO as an entertaining and collaborative SLG environment, as well as what facilitates different forms of collaboration and collaborative game play in DQO. A companion paper further explores collaboration forms and affordances found in DQ and DQO, individually and collectively [Scacchi, Nideffer, and Adams 2008].

Informal Science Education through Science Learning Games

Informal Science Education (ISE) is concerned with providing and experiencing scientific concepts, methods, and devices drawn from different science disciplines in settings outside of school, where formal science education occurs. Science centers, museums, after school clubs, and public media (e.g., the *Nova* television series broadcast in the U.S over the Public Broadcasting System/PBS) are the common settings for ISE, though ISE can also occur at home in settings with family or friends. What is key to ISE is that it is elective, discretionary, and a matter of free choice in terms of the content provider, as opposed to schools whose choices may be determined by school boards or others. However, in our view, science centers that showcase interactive, hands-on exhibits are an ideal setting to deploy SLGs, as part of an overall environment for ISE that is readily accessible to a large public audience.

---

[2] http://www.nap.edu/readingroom/books/nses/overview.html. These standards are not part of recent U.S. Federal initiatives like "No Child Left Behind" nor are they the basis for testing scientific knowledge by school grade. Instead, they focus on identifying for teachers, parents, and others what scientific concepts and practices students should be taught and learned (hopefully) in order to become scientifically literate citizens through their K-12 education. Students who excel or become enthusiastic learners of such materials may then be prepared for college level study and a career in a science, technology, engineering, or mathematical field.

SLGs are a small and mostly marginalized genre of computer games when one looks at the international computer game industry. No companies appear to be making millions of dollars from their best-selling SLGs. In fact, most of the large, well-known computer game companies avoid developing games that are envisioned as "educational" and targeted to specific age-skill groups. Instead, they more often seek to develop games that are fun, entertaining, and engaging, as well as focused on fantasy worlds, rather than on education and academic subjects. Subsequently, there is comparatively little industry interest in developing and deploying educational games in general, and SLGs in particular. However, as some game scholars and educational theorists have observed, many computer games succeed because they are great learning environments that embody both classic and modern theories of constructivist learning, self-identity through role play, reflective thinking, domain-specific specialist language skills, and multi-player socialization [Bainbridge 2007, Gee 2003, Shaffer 2006].

DinoQuest Online

The DinoQuest Online venue—The DQO venue is a publicly available Web site that downloads a Flash-based DQO game engine needed to play the game. The DQO game engine dynamically loads the content associated with each game module. DQO currently supports 13 game modules. Each module is a game, and the modules are partially ordered and game play results/knowledge are accumulative. The DQO game modules provide a set of simulated environment, some literal, other strictly conceptual. Figure 2 provides a view of the in-game home for DQO that appears as a multi-media computing laboratory or collaboratory [cf. Collabs 2008, Teasley and Wolensky 2001]. In the figure, the large multi-panel wall display serves as the in-game interface for "connecting" to remote collaboratories in geographic locations. Selecting one of these collaboratory panels transitions the user to the associated game modules. The large map display is the "DinoSphere" which is a higher level, multi-player game space that is accessible only after completing the other game modules. The doors to the right take the user to "MyLab", which is the user's private in-game laboratory office where their research points and other objects collected through DQO are kept for later use. The computer screen in the foreground is an interface to an embedded multi-media presentation from an avatar. Most of the 13 game modules can be played by a single user, but based on observations at the DSC, children often play DQO with an adult/parent companion who wants to share the game play experience, engage the child player with a discussion about game play, or seek an explanation from the child about what's going on in the game (more often than not, the child needs to explain how the game works to the parent/adult who doesn't usually play computer games).

DQO game environment—DQO represents a contemporary game platform. It is coded in Flash 8, which runs in most commonly available Web browsers (e.g., Internet Explorer, Firefox, Safari). It is accessed from a single Web site (www.DQOnline.org), which in turn downloads the DQO game engine into the user's Web browser, which in turn downloads each game module and its content on user demand. Many families and school groups access and run the DQO game environment on a desktop or laptop computer, as DQO does not require high-end microprocessors, graphics accelerator cards, or the like. Accordingly, the design of the DQO game environment was conceived to enable the largest possible audience of end users or players, including those who may have older, less powerful computers, which includes many under-privileged schools.

Multi-genre game design—As previously indicated, DQO consists of 13 game modules. Collectively, they take a player about 3-5 hours to play to completion. However, individual game modules vary in the duration, exposition of life science concepts, and game genre. For example, DQO game modules includes games drawn from quest, design/simulation, puzzle, and mini-game genres. However, it may also be fair to say that these games can individually or collectively be viewed as "casual games" that can be started, played for a brief period, stopped, and re-started later. However, game scores and research points earned persist across game play sessions, as long as the same user (identifier) is playing.

Embedded multi-media content—DQO incorporates multi-media assets originally created for presentation at the DSC. Figure 4 shows an example of an embedded video file that is played on command, and provides a brief explanation of the goals and levels found in DQO. Use of these in-game characters DQO enables a dual coding of the role models with SLG constructs [Rieber 2005] and creates a sense of continuity in content and play experience in an online environment.

Embedded tutorials for teachers and parents—Gee [2003] reports that children who learn to play games in such a manner often acquire deep knowledge of the in-game specialist language, terminology, and game play moves that are difficult to determine by a competent adult just by reading a game manual. However, in order to help satisfy the requests from parents, teachers, and other educators, we added a series of embedded tutorials and in-context explanations to help teachers and parents better understand what their children may already know. Figure 5 provides a display of in-game help that is part of such a tutorial for one of the game modules. Beyond this, as DQO players progress from game module to module, DQO also displays interstitial (and stylized) text panels that provide further contextual information about some of the underlying scientific concepts or discoveries that are recreated in the game. These interstitial images (or cut scenes) also serve to occupy the player group (e.g., child and parent) with a simple diversion while the next game module in being downloaded and readied for play.

Contemporary game play practices used to elucidate life science concepts—SLGs, as games, need to be more than just interactive presentation of scientific concepts, or simulations of scientific practices or processes. As such, we sought to find way to utilize both original and familiar game play mechanisms and play practices in developing each of the DQO game modules. For example, in Figure 6, we see a view of the ecological relationships game module within DQO that enables play with prey-predator and food chain relationships. This module utilizes a "Tetris" style of game play, where a configuration of ecological elements (carnivores/predators, herbivores/prey, and plants) can be rotated as they move from left to right to match up with configurations that have already been anchored, in order to maximize the matches (e.g., carnivores prey on herbivores, herbivores prey on plants, unmatched carnivores die and help nuture plants). As such, we (and many adult players familiar with Tetris games) find this game is both familiar to play, yet at the same time, presents basic life science concepts by repurposing contemporary game mechanisms and practices.

Multi-person game play—As we have indicated above, it is possible for an individual to play DQO without others. Beyond this, DQO also features a final level game module, DinoSphere, which is a multi-player or multi-character game module. In this module, player specify and configure a dinosaur of their choosing, using the resources and points they have earned from previous game play. DinoSphere features four ecological niches that serve as simulated physical world environments where different dinosaurs must survive or co-habitate. As players by this point have already learned about life science concepts like prey-predater relationships, then the quickly realize small predators (e.g., raptors) individually are not a threat to larger prey (stegosaurus), unless they can find other similar predators who can then collectively act to surround and overwhelm a larger prey. Figure 7 provides a view of a forest ecological niche within DinoSphere where one small raptor seeks to engage a larger stegosaurus as prey, but without success.

Discussion and planned enhancements to DQO

The first topic of discussion is whether the DQO games are fun to play. Since fun may be in the mind of the player, we can report results from sustained informal observations (along with a multitude of DSC administered survey questionnaires and interviews) that the quick and simple answer is: yes, they are fun to play, but each is fun in a different way. Second, do the players learn anything useful about scientific inquiry or life science? Again based on the same instrumentality for observation, the quick and simple answer is yes, though what is learned across DQO games is different. In both situations, DQO is a game environment played in an online, Web-based venue where other people may be involved in play, but their involvement may be centered around interaction at the human-computer interface or through in-game dinosaur characters foraging in a simulated ecological niche. So we expect that what's fun and what's learned will be different, but we continue to seek to understand how and why they are different.

First, reflecting the diversity of people (students, parents, and others) who visit DSC, we seek to provide multi-lingual game play user interfaces for DQO in languages such as Spanish and Korean. Actually, we developed DQO with internationalization and localization as part of the design and implementation scheme, so provision of multi-lingual support is primary one of adding and replacing corresponding in-game textual content across languages.

Second, following from this, we seek to provide multi-national deployments for DQO to non-English speaking venues. Dinosaur themed interactive science exhibits are being developed in areas like Mexico, Latin America, and South Korea. Though DQO was designed with California Science Education Standards in mind, our correspondence with colleagues in those areas indicates such standards are acceptable as a starting point.

Third, we seek to expand the multi-player capabilities of the DQO DinoSphere to accommodate more MMOG services amd game play modes. Our intent is to add such capabilities to the highest levels of DQO-DinoSphere game play, so that existing game content and play experience will be minimally affected. The wisdom of this choice remains to be seen and realized.

Last, our original goals included making DQO a networked SLG environment that could be built from open source software, support open content artwork, and accommodate a controlled interface to the Web of open and current scientific research related to paleontology and paleobiology. None of this has been realized, and the technical choices that we have invested will limit what we can do to realize these goals. Nonetheless, they remain part of our long-term goal, and we look forward to opportunities that will enable to develop more collaborative SLGs in other scientific domains and for other public audiences who want informal science education experiences and resources.

Conclusions

In this paper, we described some of the concepts and results that arose from the development and deployment of a large-scale collaborative science learning game environment called DinoQuest Online. DQO provides an entertaining experience and approach to informal science education, as well as matching California/National Science Education Standards. As noted, games for helping school-age children to learn about science (or more specifically, life science) are not a focus of the global computer game industry, yet we believe it represents an important and under-served community of potential game players and others (parents, teachers) who want to informally collaborate in and around such a science learning game environment. Subsequently, we identified and examined different collaborative group forms that emerged to play DQO, as well as the affordances that help facilitate collaborative game play. Along the way we provided examples of the collaborative groups and game play from DQO.

In closing, we welcome participants of the First IFIP Entertainment Computing Symposium to register and play one or more of the DinoQuest Online game modules found starting at http://www.DQOnline.org. DQO will provide experiences for collaborative games and game play which can last for 3-5 hours in total.

Acknowledgements: Development of DinoQuest Online was supported by the Discovery Science Center, its members, and many governmental and corporate sponsors. Recent R&D projects at the UCGameLab are supported with contracts and grants from the Digital Industry Promotion Agency (DIP) in Daegu, South Korea, Intel Research, California Institute for Telecommunications and Information Technology (Calit2), and others. No endorsement implied. Some of the other participants involved in the development of DinoQuest Online include Alex Szeto (DQO game art and programming), Calvin Lee (DQO database programming), Janet Yamaguchi (California Science Education Standards, and Education Programs at DSC), and Celia Pearce (design contributions).

References

Allison-Bunnell, S. and Schaller, D.T. (2005). From the Physical to the Virtual: Bringing Free-Choice Science Education Online, in L. Tan and R. Subramanian (eds.), *E-Learning and Virtual Science Centers*, 163-189, Hershey, PA, IGI Global Publishing, 2005.

Bainbridge, W.S. (2007). The Scientific Research Potential of Virtual Worlds, *Science*, 317, 472-476.

Bogost, I. (2007). *Persuasive Games: The Expressive Power of Videogames*, MIT Press, Cambridge, MA.

Collabs, (2008). The Science of Collaboratories, http://www.scienceofcollaboratories.org/

DSC, (2008). Discovery Science Center, Santa Ana, CA. http://www/discoverycube.org

Gee, J.P. (2003). *What Computer Games Have To Teach Us About Learning and Literacy,* Palgrave Macmillan, New York.

Koster, R. (2004). *A Theory of Fun for Game Design*, Paraglyph Press.

LaFarge, A. and Nideffer, R. (2002). Shift-Ctrl: Computer, Games, and Art, *Leonardo: A Journal of Art, Science, and Technology*. MIT Press. 35(1), 5-13, Winter.

Malone, T. and Lepper, M.R. (1987). Making Learning Fun: A taxonomy of intrinsic motivations for learning, in R.E. Snow and M.J. Farr, *Aptitude, Learning, and Instruction III: Conative and Affective Process Analyses*, 223-253, Erlbaum, Hillsdale, NJ.

Nardi, B. and Harris, J. (2006). Strangers and Friends: Collaborative Play in World of Warcraft, *Proc. 2006 Conf. Computer Support Cooperative Work (CSCW'06)*, 149-158, Banff, Canada, ACM Press.

Nideffer, R. (2002). *PROXY*, The Whitney Museum Portal to Net Art, http://artport.whitney.org/exhibitions/biennial2002/nideffer.shtml.

Nideffer, R. (2006). *unexceptional.net*, http://transliteracies.english.ucsb.edu/post/research-project/project-members/robert-nideffer

Nideffer, R. (2007). Game Engines as Embedded Systems, in V. Vesna (ed.), *Database Aesthetics: Art in the Age of Information Overflow*. University of Minnesota Press. Minneapolis, Minnesota.

Rieber, L.P. (2005). Multimedia Learning in Games, Simulations, and Microworlds, in R.E. Mayer (ed.), *The Cambridge Handbook of Multimedia Learning*, Cambridge University Press, Cambridge, UK.

Salen, K. and Zimmerman, E. (2003). *Rules of Play: Game Design Fundamentals*, MIT Press.

Scacchi, W. (2004). Free/Open Source Software Development Practices in the Computer Game Community, *IEEE Software*, 21(1), 59-67, January/February 2004.

Scacchi, W. and Adams, J. (2007). Recent Developments in Science Learning Games for Informal Science Education, presentation at *Games, Learning, and Society: 3.0*, Madison, WI. July.

Scacchi, W., Nideffer, R., and Adams, J. (2008). Collaborative Game Environments for Informal Science Education: DinoQuest and DinoQuest Online, *2008 Collaboration Technologies and Systems Symposium*, Irvine, CA (submitted for publication).
Shaffer, D. W. (2006). *How Computer Games Help Children Learn*, Palgrave Macmillan, New York.

Teasley, S., & Wolensky, S. (2001) Scientific collaborations at a distance. *Science*, 292, 2254-2255.

UCGameLab, (2008). Game Culture and Technology Laboratory, University of California, Irvine, Irvine, CA. http://www.UCGameLab.net

WDIL (2008). *Web Designs for Interactive Learning*, http://www.wdil.org/

Figure 1. DinoQuest Physical Site.

Figure 2. DinoQuest Online in-game home.

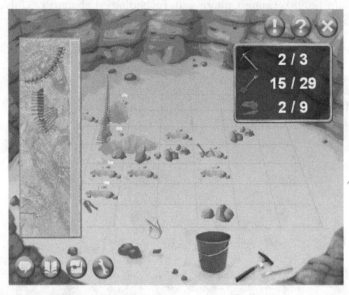

Figure 3. The Fossil Dig Pit game module showing different in-game user controls (hand, pick, shovel) and a dashboard indicating resource utilization (number of possible uses of the pick and shovel).

Figure 4. An in-game scene in DQO with an embedded video displaying featuring an in-character that introduces and explains DQO's goals and levels.

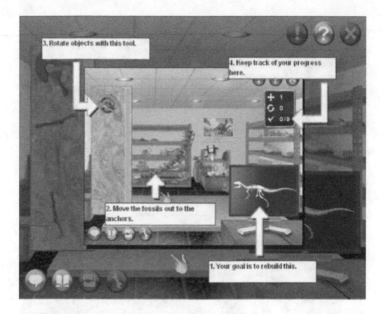

Figure 5. An in-game view of a teacher/parent tutorial explaining the goal and process for playing this DQO game module (reconstructing fossilized skeletal bones collected in the Fossil dig pit module).

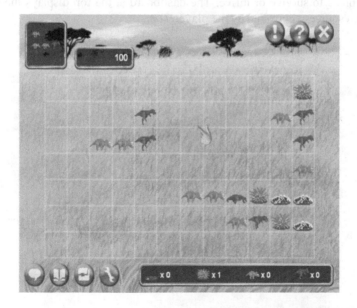

Figure 6. A Tetris-like game for matching ecological relationships like prey-predator and food chains.

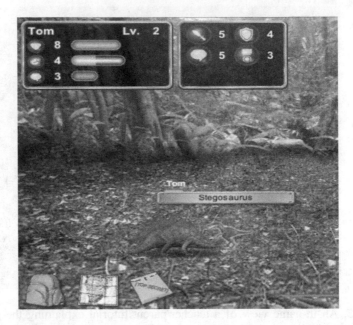

Figure 7. A scene from the DQO module, DinoSphere, where multiple players or in-game characters (e.g., stegosaurus and raptor) can interact in a simulated ecological niche to survive or thrive. The dashboard at the top displays the status of various resources controlled by the player *Tom*.

Construction and Evaluation of a Robot Dance System

Kuniya Shinozaki[1], Akitsugu Iwatani[2], and Ryohei Nakatsu[3]

[1]Kwansei Gakuin University, School of Science and Technology
2-1 Gakuen, Sanda Japan, 669-1337
scbc0052@kwansei.ac.jp

[2]Universal Studios Japan
Osaka, Japan
Iwatani@nirvana.ne.jp

[3]National University of Singapore, Interactive & Digital Media Institute
Block E3A, #02-04, 7 Engineering Drive 1, Singapore 11774
idmdir@nus.edu.sg

Abstract Dance is one form of entertainment where physical movement is the key factor. The main reason why robots are experiencing a kind of "boom" is that they have a physical body. We propose a robot dance system that combines these two elements. First, various factors concerning entertainment and dance are studied. Then we propose the dance system by robot using motion unit and the synthetic rule referring the speech synthesis. Also we describe the details of the system by focusing on its software functions. Finally we show the evaluation results of robot dance performances.

1 Introduction

The research and development of various kinds of robots is actively being carried out, especially in Japan [1][2][3][4][5]. Several reasons explain the current robot boom. One main reason is that robots have physical bodies, and so human-robot interaction extends beyond human-computer interaction.

Although in the future these robots are expected to support various aspects of our daily life, so far their capabilities are very limited. At present, installing such a task in robots remains very difficult. To break through such a situation, entertainment might be a good application area for robots.

Developing a dancing robot would be remarkable from various points of view. First, it might become a new form of entertainment, activates both the body and brain. Watching humans dance is already one established type of entertainment.

Please use the following format when citing this chapter:

Shinozaki, K., Iwatani, A. and Nakatsu, R., 2008, in IFIP International Federation for Information Processing, Volume 279; *New Frontiers for Entertainment Computing*; Paolo Ciancarini, Ryohei Nakatsu, Matthias Rauterberg, Marco Roccetti; (Boston: Springer), pp. 83–94.

Second, we might develop a new type of communication with computers, because dance can be considered one of the most sophisticated nonverbal communication methods.

Based on the above considerations we started to research dancing robots. In this paper we clarify the relationship among entertainment, humans, and robots and propose a robot dance system by robot using motion unit and the synthetic rule referring the speech synthesis. Also we will describe an evaluation experiment carried out to test this basic concept's feasibility.

2 Dance Entertainment and Robots

2.1 Entertainment

The role of entertainment in our daily life is very important. It offers relaxation and thus contributes to our mental health. Many aspects concerning entertainment must be considered and discussed [6]. One of the most important may be the existence of two sides: entertainer and audience. Although these two sides change positions depending on the case, the existence of performers and spectators is an absolute prerequisite for entertainment. Many entertainments have both entertainer and spectator characteristics. In the case of dance, people sometimes go to theaters to watch good dance performances, and they sometimes go to dance clubs or discos to dance themselves.

Furthermore, when viewed from a different aspect entertainment can be classified into two types. One is a real-time type that includes performers or entertainers performing live in front of an audience. Good examples include plays and/or concerts. Another is the non-real-time type; reading books and watching movies are good examples.

Following this classification, dance basically belongs to the real-time type of entertainment. For robot dancing, however, as described later, its position is somewhat special.

2.2 Dance Robot

One main reason why we choose dance as an entertainment for robots is that dance is quite sophisticated [7]. Based on the considerations described above, what is the role of robots in dance entertainment? Dance robots allow us to become both entertainers and spectators. When watching a robot dance, we are spectators. On the other side, many people will probably want to install dance motions on their robots and show these actions to others. In this case they are entertainers. For the classification between real-time and non-real-time entertainment, dance robots also have significant characteristics. If we want to show people the robot dance, we have to install the dance actions beforehand, meaning that the robot dance is non-real-time entertainment. At the same time, by developing interactive capabilities, the robot would show impromptu dancing behaviors. For example, it could change the dance depending on audience requests. Or it could sense the audience mood and could adopt its dancing behaviors to reflect the sensor results. A dance robot could provide flexible entertainment that ranges between real-time and non-real-time entertainment.

3 Dance Robot System

3.1 Basic Concept

Based on the above considerations we want to develop a system that can generate various dance motions. Since different dance genres exist, it is necessary to restrict dance genres to a specific one. Then the system would generate various dance motions by selecting several basic dance motions and by concatenating them. This basic idea resembles text-to-speech synthesis (TTS) [8], where by restricting the language to be synthesized and by selecting a basic speech unit, any kind of text described by the language can be generated. The following is the basic concept adopted in TTS:

(1) Speech consists of a concatenation of basic speech units.

(2) Selection of the speech unit is crucial.

(3) Connection of speech units is also crucial.

As basic speech units, various basic units such as phonemes, phoneme pairs, CV (consonant-vowel concatenation), CVC, VCV and so on have been studied [8]. Based on research of the last several decades, phonemes including variations that depend on previous and following phonemes are widely used as speech units. Taking these situations into consideration, the basic concept of dance generation is as follows:

(1) We restrict the generated dance to a specific genre.

(2) All dance motions consist of a concatenation of several basic dance motions.

(3) Deciding what to select dance units as basic dance motions is very important.

(4) Connecting dance units is crucial.

(5) Also it is crucial how to express a dance unit as robot motion.
In the following sections, we answer the above questions.

3.2 Dance Genre

For basic dance motions, there are several researches on classic ballet [9]. The classification of ballet motions is based on several leg positions and movements called steps. Although each leg position and step has its own name, basically no rules describe the details of whole body motions. We chose hip-hop as the dance genre because all of its dance steps and motions are classified into several categories, so it is easier to handle the whole body motions of hip-hop than ballet.

3.3 Dance Unit

Next we must decide the basic unit for dance motions. As described above, since each hip-hop step/body motion has its own name, it can be selected as a dance unit. However, it is difficult for an amateur to extract them from continuous dance motions. Therefore we collaborated with a professional dancer to simplify the extraction of basic motions from continuous dance motions. In addition, when constructing robot motions based on human motions, we must deform complicated human motions into rather simple robot motions. In this deformation process, a professional dancer's advice is also of great help.

3.4 Concatenation of Dance Units

The next question is how to connect each motion unit. One method interpolates the last posture of the previous motion and the first posture of the next motion. The difficulty in the case of a dancing robot is how to connect these two motions and prevent the robot from falling down. We introduced a method in which a neutral posture represented by a standing still pose is used as a transition posture between two dance units. In this case developing an algorithm is unnecessary to generate a transitional motion that connects two different motions.

3.5 Realization of Robot Dance Motion

The next issue is transforming human dance motions into the motions of robots. One common method adopts a motion capture system that is used to generate the motion of CG characters. For a robot, however, due to the limitations of the degree of freedom at each joint, directly transforming the motion captured by the system into robot motion does not work well. Research that transforms captured motions into robot motions is described in [10] that treats a Japanese traditional dance whose motions include legs moving slowly and smoothly front/back and left/right instead of dynamically. In this case it is relatively easy to maintain balance. However, hip-hop motions include dynamic body motions, and therefore it is difficult to maintain balance. Taking these situations into considerations, we chose a method where each motion unit extracted from continuous motion is transformed manually.

3.6 System Architecture

Based on the above considerations, we constructed the first prototype of a robot dance system, as shown in Fig. 1, that consists of dance unit sequence generation, a dance unit database, and dance unit concatenation.

(1) Dance unit database

A large amount of dance units are stored here; each one corresponds to a basic short dance motion and is expressed as robot motion data.

(2) Dance unit sequence generation

An input data that expresses a dance motion is analyzed and converted into a sequence of dance units by this part. At the present stage a sequence of dance units is directly used as input data and fed into the system.

(3) Dance unit concatenation

As is described in 3.4, a neutral posture is introduced as an intermediate posture between two dance units, and therefore, they can be easily connected.

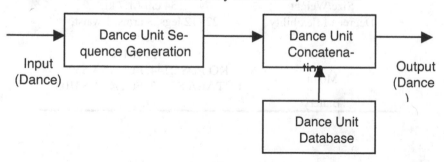

Fig. 1 Structure of dance robot system

4 System Development and Evaluation

4.1 Humanoid Robot

From the several humanoid robots already available on the market, we selected a humanoid robot developed by Nirvana Technology [11] and installed dance motions on it. Figure 2 shows its appearance, and Table 1 shows its basic specifications. Various robot motions can be designed and produced on PC using a "motion editor" realized by motion making and editing software.

Fig. 2 Humanoid robot

Table 1 Specifications of humanoid robot

Size/Weight	34 cm / 1.7 kg
Degree of flexibility	22 (12 legs, 8 arms, 1 waist, 1 head)
CPU	SH2/7047F
Motor	KO PDS-2144, FUTABA S3003, FUTABA S3102, FUTABA S3103
Battery	DC6V

4.2 Development of Dance Unit Database

As described above, we collaborated with a dancer to develop a dance unit database and conducted the following database generation:

(1) First, a typical hip-hop motion of several minutes long was recorded.

(2) Then we observed and discussed the dance sequence and selected about 60 motions as dance units that included almost all the representative hip-hop motions.

(3) We asked the dancer to separately perform each motion corresponding to each dance unit and recorded it. At the same time we asked him to start each dance motion from a "natural standing posture" and to finish in the same posture.

(4) By watching each dance motion being performed, we tried to create a robot dance motion that corresponds to human dance motion using motion editor.

4.3 Evaluation of Robot Dancing

Using the system described above we carried out simple evaluation experiments.

4.3.1 Comparison of the two types of robot dance units

We evaluated the two types of dance units; one was generated by the professional dancer (type 1) and the other by non-experts (type 2). First we classified all the dance motions into three categories according to the complications of the motions; primary, intermediate, and advanced. And we selected one representative motion for each category. These dance motions are "Lock"(primary), "Rolling Arm" (intermediate), and "Club"(advanced). Then we generated two types of robot dance motions for each of these motions.

Ten subjects were asked to compare these two types of robot dance motions by giving a score ranging from 1 to 5 to each dance motion (1 is the worst and 5 is the best). Figure 3 shows the comparison between the two types of dance motions; robot dance motions developed by the dancer himself (type 1) and those developed by non-experts (type 2) for three kinds of motions; (a) Lock, (b) Rolling arm, and (c) Crab. Also the live dance motions performed by the dancer is shown as references. Figure 4 shows the evaluation results for each of the three kinds of motions. The evaluation result and the consideration for each motion are described below.

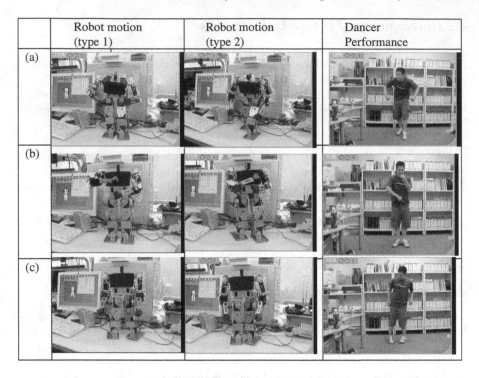

	Robot motion (type 1)	Robot motion (type 2)	Dancer Performance
(a)			
(b)			
(c)			

Fig. 3 Comparison of three dance motions

(1) Lock

This is a repeating motion of moving and stopping like being locked. In this move the sharpness of stopping motion is an important factor as a dance. For "sharpness," type 1 motion (motion designed by a professional dancer) obtained the higher score than type 2 (motions designed by non-experts) as expected. On the other hand, for such evaluation items as "exciting," "wonder," and "smooth," the type 2 motion got higher scores than the type 1 motion. It seems that the stop-and-go motion designed by the dancer was judged awkward by the subjects.

(2) Rolling arm

This is a motion of moving body while turning arms smoothly. For the sharpness, the type 1 motion obtained higher score than the type 2. But for other evaluation items, the type 2 motions generally got slightly higher scores. Especially for "smooth" type 2 received much higher scores against type 1. Originally this motion contains a step raising legs, and the type 1 motion precisely simulates this process and in the case of sharpness it worked well and obtained the high score. On the other hand, the type 2 motion achieves this move by sliding legs without raising legs. As a result, it was judged that the type 2 motion looked smoother than the type 1, and this gave a influence to the result of smoothness evaluation and others.

(3) Crab

This motion is a move peculiar to the Hip-hop dance. It includes a move of sliding legs sideways without raising them and fixing their backside on floor and thus moving the body sideways. The motion designed by the professional dancer (type 1) receives higher scores than the motion designed by non-expert (type 2) for almost all evaluation items. Especially, important evaluation items for this move such as "exciting," "wonder," and "smooth," the type 1 obtains fairly higher evaluation scores than the type 2.

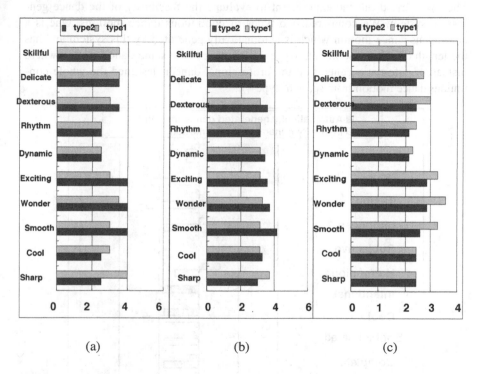

(a)   (b)   (c)

Fig. 4 Evaluation results for three kinds of motions

These result shows that as the robot dance motions become more complex, they can get higher scores. The reason for this would be that the professional dancer understands so well the characteristics of each dance motion and his knowledge and now-how is reflected on the robot dance motion. Even though it does not appear so well in the case of simple motions, this characteristic reveals itself in the case of complicated motions. On the other hand, the motion designed by non-expert (type 2) obtained higher evaluation scores than the type 1 for simple motions. The explanation for this would be that the subjects got good impressions for the over-actions and the unstableness that the type 2 motions generally contain and express themselves. Contrarily, the type 1 motions designed by a professional dancer are sophisticated without containing such over-action nor unstableness. This characteristic sometimes leads to rather low evaluation scores as the subjects are non-expert of dances and thus could not understand the details of the dance motions where the knowledge and now-how of the professional are stored.

4.3.2 Evaluation of the continuous dance motion

Then we carried out the experiment to evaluate the feasibility of the dance generation system. We compared two types of continuous dance motions. One is a continuous dance motion which is automatically generated by this system and has the length of about one minute (type 3). Another is the same dance motion where instead of automatic generation the professional dancer designed the whole continuous dance motion from scratch (type 4).

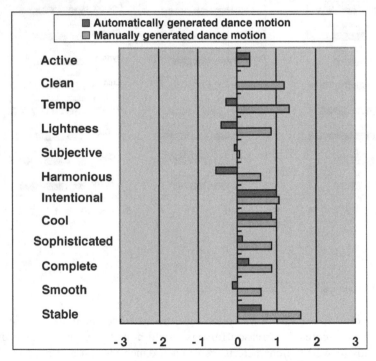

Fig. 5 Comparison between automatically generated motions and manually generated motions

For evaluation twelve items generally used for the sensibility evaluation such as "stable," "soft", "smooth," and so on were selected. Each evaluation item has a seven level score ranging from -3 to 3. For example, for the evaluation item "stable" the 0 means neutral, 3 means very stable, and -3 is very unstable. Figure 5 shows the evaluation result. The type 4 obtained fairly good results for most of the evaluation items. This means that the evaluation items were fairly well selected. Generally the dance motion generated by this dance generation system (type 3) obtained lower evaluation scores than the type 4 motion. Especially, for such evaluation items as "harmony," "lightness," and "tempo, " the type 3 motion obtained minus evaluation scores. This is because the subject felt unnaturalness due to the neutral posture effect used to connect the two dance units. This means that the system still needs further improvement to generate continuous dance motion, especially for the connection of two dance units. At the same time, however, the type 3 motion got plus scores for "stability", "cool", and "intentional." Especially for "cool" and "intentional" the evaluation results are almost as high as the results of the type 4 motion. This shows that the continuous dance motion generated by this system would be effective as far as it is used as a performance even at the present stage.

The difference between type 3 and type 4 motions are that in the case of type 3 motion it goes back to a neutral position at the point of the dance unit connection. It is necessary to improve this point by introducing better neutral posture or introducing multiple neutral postures.

5 Conclusion

In this paper we proposed a dance robot system as a new application area for humanoid robots. We clarified several distinctive entertainment characteristics and investigated the role of robots in entertainment.

Based on these basic considerations we proposed a dance robot system in which a humanoid robot performs various dance motions. We hypothesized that any dance motion consists of a concatenation of short dance motions called dance units. This basic idea was imported from TTS, where any text can be converted into speech by concatenating short basic speech called speech units. Based on this basic idea, we collaborated with a professional dancer. After recording and analyzing his hip-hop dancing, we extracted about sixty dance units and converted them into the motions of a humanoid robot. By concatenating these dance units we found that a huge amount of dance variations for the hip-hop genre could be achieved.

Then we carried out two types of evaluation experiments. First we compared dance motions designed by the professional dancer and the ones by non-experts of dancing. We found that as the dance motions become more complicated and sophisticated, the dance motions by the dancer got higher evaluation results. Then we compared a continuous dance motion automatically generated by this system and one fully manually designed. Although the automatically generated dance got lower evaluation results, for some evaluation items it got almost the same scores.

This means that this system is promising from a point of automatic dance generation. Further studies must address the following issues. First we have to investigate how many dance units are enough to generate any type of hip-hop dance. Also we have to investigate the feasibility of a neutral posture that connects two dance units. As only one type of neutral posture was used so far, still there is some unnaturalness for the automatically generated continuous dance motion. We expect that by introducing several other neutral postures, continuous dance motions achieved by the robot would become more natural.

References

1. Golubovic, D., Li, B., and Hu, H. A Hybrid Software Platform for Sony AIBO Robots. (2003). *RoboCup 2003: Robot Soccer World Cup* VII, 478-486.
2. Ishimura, T., Kato, T., Oda, T., and Ohashi, T. An Open Robot Simulator Environment. (2003). *RoboCup 2003: Robot Soccer World Cup* VII, 621-627
3. Kerepesi, A., Kubinyi, E., Jonsson, G. K., Magnusson, M. S., and Kiklosi, A. Behavioural Comparison of Human-Animal (Dog) and Human-Robot (AIBO) Interactions. (2006). *Behavioural Processes*, Vol. 73, No.1, 92-99.
4. Wama, T., Higuchi, M., Sakamoto, H., and Nakatsu, R. Realization of Tai-chi Motion Using a Humanoid Robot. (2004). *Entertainment Computing*, Springer LNCS, 14-19.
5. http://www.expo2005.or.jp/en/index.html
6. Callois, R. *Les Jeux et les Hommes*. (1958). Paris: Callimard.
7. Laban, R. *The Mastery of Movement*. (1980). Macdonald and Evans; 4th ed., revised and enlarged edition.
8. Kleijn, W. B. and Paliwal, K. K. (ed.), *Speech Coding and Synthesis*. (1995). Elsevier.
9. Lee, C. *Ballet in Western Culture: A History of Its Origins and Evolution*. (2002). Routledge, London.
10. Nakaoka, S., Nakazawa, A., Yokoi, K., Hirukawa, H., and Ikeuchi, K. Generating Whole Body Motions for a Biped Humanoid Robot from Captured Human Dances. (2003). *IEEE 2003 International Conference on Robotics and Automation*.
11. http://www.nirvana.ne.jp/

Context-aware fun and games with Bluetooth

Andy Sloane and Chris Dennett

School of Computing and IT, University of Wolverhampton, UK

A.Sloane@wlv.ac.uk, C.Dennett@wlv.ac.uk.

Abstract   Bluetooth-enabled devices are everywhere and in everyday use by a
             large number of mobile phone users. Harnessing this communication
             channel for a context-aware system has proved to be a useful step
             forward in providing simple games, fun events and targeted advertis-
             ing based on the awareness of the user's location. As part of a wider
             project the authors have produced a system that allows users to
             download information based on Global positioning (GPS) inputs on
             moving server platforms within public transport. The project has also
             tied "context" to information to send information to users via the
             same platform based in a static system for applications such as guided
             trails and tours in open spaces.

1. Introduction

The system outlined here has two distinct implementations:

1. A system designed to inhabit a mobile space such as a train, tram or bus
2. A system which delivers information based on a user's location in relation to a static system which delivers information with embedded context.

Using Bluetooth is a cost-effective means of providing a delivery system for
these mobile information services. The information that can be provided is from a
range of multimedia, interactive gaming and other active content. Tie this to the
ability to interact with the outside environment via a GPS input and the information and gaming experience can be made "context-aware".

Based on a system [1] used for e-learning support the Bluetooth server design
is outlined below. Using this design enabled the project to deliver information
based on location information from a GPS input to the server and to frequently

Please use the following format when citing this chapter:

Sloane, A. and Dennett, C., 2008, in IFIP International Federation for Information Processing, Volume 279; *New Frontiers for
Entertainment Computing*; Paolo Ciancarini, Ryohei Nakatsu, Matthias Rauterberg, Marco Roccetti; (Boston: Springer), pp. 95–104.

update the information on the mobile system when in proximity to the project's wireless network.

The purposes of the project were:

- To provide a means of up-to-date information to travellers or tourists
- To provide games and fun items to users via a commonly available platform (mobile phone)
- To provide more serious information such as health education and newsflashes
- To assist users in their travel arrangements
- To act as a means of advertising in a timely and context-driven scenario
- To provide information from static servers with embedded context for later use.

These two different context-based systems required different design strategies and different engagement with the user's device. The use of short bursts of information to the users in a mobile setting (e.g. on a bus or tram) was made possible by the constant "availability" of the users during the journey. Longer bursts of information in the static system were used as the users could engage with the system while entering the experience e.g. buying tickets.

Both systems have been deployed in live environments, with restricted access devices having to be specified (variability of the features and compatibility of the variety of mobile phone platforms does not allow a complete range to be targeted easily), but the intention is to widen the system to cater for more user devices to enable as wide a participation as possible. Other similar systems in the past [2] have used Bluetooth as a location finding tool – this system relies on GPS to do that and only uses Bluetooth as a delivery mechanism it is, therefore restricted. The mobile system relying on an antenna input which does not have too many problems, but the static system uses the phone's own GPS system to deliver context/location information and this relies on the availability of signal in the area of the delivery zone. (Initial "urban canyon" problems restricted the usability of location-driven application in some areas such as the City Centre).

2. The delivery system

The system makes use of inexpensive and widely available Bluetooth Universal Serial Bus (USB) 'dongles', and open source software to provide a communications link between the "system" and "users" that requires nothing else, other than a computer, to create a transmission hub or information server.

2.1 Bluetooth Technology in Brief

Bluetooth is a licence-free communications protocol transmitting in the Industrial, Scientific and Medical band and designed for short range ad-hoc networking. Its operation in this band means that it competes with transmissions of all other licence-free short-range systems such as wireless network access points (Wi-Fi). Originally developed by Ericsson in 1994, the standard is now under the control of the Bluetooth Special Interest Group (SIG) [3]. The technology first came to prominence (and is still most commonly associated) with the provision of wireless headsets for mobile phones, but has since been used in a multitude of applications from wireless computer mice to streaming audio.

As an outline, the Bluetooth v1.2 transmission system uses spread-spectrum techniques to reduce the effect of other technologies working in the same band (Wi-Fi being a prime example) on transmitted packets. Transmitting on one frequency for such a short amount of time means that multiple packets are less likely to encounter distortion and there is therefore a reduced need for error control overhead, although a rate 1/3 repetition code and a rate 2/3 block code are available as well as Automatic Repeat Request (ARQ). To further reduce the likelihood of interference, problem frequencies (for instance, those used by static wireless transmitters) are avoided by the systems adaptive algorithm which takes note of frequencies that regularly cause interference to Bluetooth transmission and avoids them for future packet transmissions. Gaussian Frequency Shift Keying (GFSK), a simple and robust digital modulation technique is used for data transmission in Bluetooth v1.2. To increase data throughput, Bluetooth v2.0 uses GFSK only for header information, favouring the increased rate of Quadrature Phase Shift Keying (QPSK), with a guard and synchronisation word, for the payload. This payload rate is further increased through the use of 8-PSK for the Enhanced Data Rate (EDR) that has recently come to market. The ad-hoc network can take on one of two forms. In the first instance, where less than eight devices are present, a *piconet* is formed. In this situation, one device becomes the master and the others become slaves. All of these devices can communicate with one another simultaneously. If more devices are present, or come within range, slaves can act as masters in other piconets, thus forming a *scatternet*.

Alongside the radio transmission standard is a range of profiles that are defined by the SIG. These specifications form the backbone to any Bluetooth software development and include profiles for basic services, such as printing and synchronisation, and more involved services, like WAP over Bluetooth and Object Exchange (OBEX).

2.2 BlueShoot

One of the goals of this project was to provide a freely available executable for other members of the community to use for further development. Therefore, the transmission software, *BlueShoot*, is built to run on a version of the Linux operating system using Python with a MySQL database to keep track of information services permitted by each device, files to be transmitted and whether they have been successfully received or not.

The software, makes use of a number of freely available libraries, primarily PyBluez [4], a Python wrapper for the official Linux Bluetooth software stack (Bluez). This library is used for device discovery. To facilitate the transmission of information to devices using OBEX, and to more easily discover the services on a device, a high-level wrapper for PyBluez and OpenOBEX, LightBlue [5] was used.

Similar systems exist in other environments such as BlueSender for windows but the use of Open Source Software allowed faster development and more flexible utilisation during the project.

2.3 Software in Practice

Whereas SMS transmission technologies require nothing more complicated than a phone number, Bluetooth devices require considerably more information. Fortunately most of this information can be obtained via the device software; it only requires that the device is made discoverable for a short time and that the correct profile is permitted without pairing. Once the device has been detected, the user device discovery can be disabled.

The most basic use of the software is transmitting particular files to chosen devices in real time. Once devices have been discovered, the system can transmit a file to a particular device, selection of devices or all devices.

The original prototype sent JPEG images as shown in Figure 1 but this has now been superseded by a richer set of data types available to phone users.

Further extensions to the project will require more extensive communication between the user's phone and the server – for example the context for interactive communication via the server and other phones for multiplayer games requires more data and context information to be stored and different profiles.

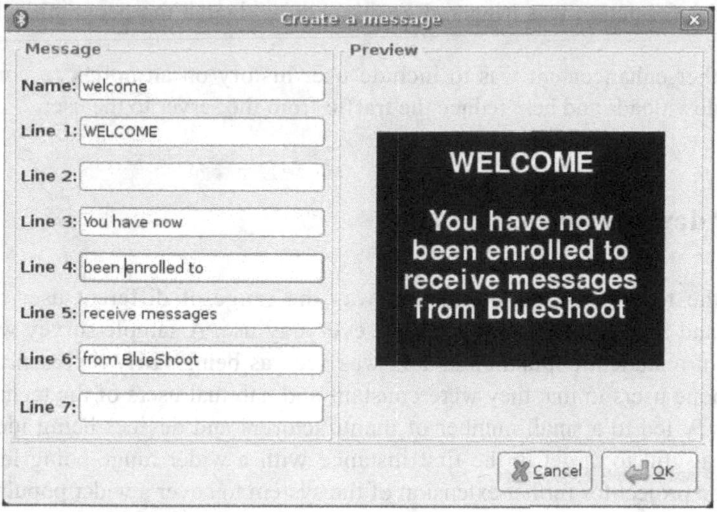

Figure 1. Message screen

2.4 Server systems

In the mobile server systems the various data inputs were:
1. Wi-Fi for updating the database on the move and
2. GPS for continuous positioning.
This enables timely data to be transmitted to users and for this to be based on the position of the server geographically. It was therefore possible to devise a system that would deliver information based on the user's location context without them having to have any GPS input on their device. This simplified the user device requirements a little and enabled the project to target a wider range of end-user devices.

The types of service developed for the system ranged from simple animated GIF files, audio files and various combined multimedia data files to active Java applications.

The static server systems were essentially simpler to construct initially as they did not require GPS input, however they did need to have a range of GPS coded trigger points to link to the informational files sent to the user's phones.

The two systems were, therefore, similar in concept but delivery was different with the mobile server system using the GPS input to trigger downloads to users from a wide range of available material; the static system downloaded a limited amount of material with embedded GPS trigger points to a user's phone so that the presented information was triggered as the user navigated the geographical space of interest.

A further enhancement was to include user history on an uplink to configure targeted downloads and help reduce the traffic from the server to the user.

3. User device considerations

One of the first problems to consider was the range of different user devices (phones and Smart-phones) which are in everyday use. A sample survey was carried out of a student population as this was seen as being fairly representative of active phone users in that they were constant and habitual users of the technology. This survey led to a small number of manufacturers and devices being identified as being useful to target in the first instance with a wider range being left until later in the project for further extension of the system to cover a wider population.

It was also felt that as the project progressed there would be technological developments of the user devices and it was only feasible to target the latest generation of devices as these would soon be widely available at little cost (the UK market being driven partly by *free* phones available on monthly air-time contracts).

The initial decision on target phone platform was to choose a Nokia N95 8GB – this provided both a modern phone with a large memory capacity and GPS capability within a reasonable size. Some of the Sony Ericsson range were also used in initial tests but the development of software was simplified by the main choice of the S60 3rd Edition operating system allowing development across a range of target phones.

Further development of the concepts and software will be to expand the range of target platforms to incorporate a wider variety of user devices but choice is left until nearer development time as the rapid obsolescence of mobile devices militates against too much investment in effort at too early a stage.

3.1 Mobile system

For the system where the server is mobile the minimum requirements of the user device were Bluetooth and support for animated GIF files. Additional support for Flash-lite and Java enabled richer content to be downloaded and used from the server.

The initial design of the software includes GPS trigger points that then allow information feeds to be downloaded to user phones at relevant points in their journey. This allows relevant advertising and other sponsored content, such as games and quizzes, to be available when the user is in the vicinity of the sponsor.

The use of a mobile server system allows a large amount of content to be retained and only relevant content delivered at the appropriate location for example as the bus approaches a restaurant it can send a targeted advertisement or a sponsored item to the enabled user phones. This approach allows both opt-in by users and better targeting of material to user requirements. This saves overloading users with too much content material; this may or not be wanted but if it is targeted by location then this allows a coarse filter to be applied. Finer filters can be applied by using an uplink to the server for user input and choice parameters.

Initial applications developed have been animated advertisements and simple games using Flash-lite.

Figure 2. A typical tour screen

3.2 Static system

The additional requirement to make the static system more useful was the inclusion of GPS within the phone. This made the choice of phones a lot more restricted but this was felt to be a temporary problem as many new phones were being predicted with inclusive GPS as an option. It was also felt that Bluetooth/GPS-enabled (Personal Digital Assistants) PDAs would be able to be included in the trials as a *proof of concept* tool but these proved to be too cumbersome to be of more than a passing interest.

The design of this static server system allowed the device to be more compact than the mobile system as generally any of the static systems were only used to deliver a limited number of content streams (mostly a single downloaded file was available at each of the project's "Bluetooth information points").

The initial design was therefore simplified to be a system that downloads a file (with embedded GPS triggers) to the user's device when they interact with the server system. The design was furthered enhanced to included interaction with the user's history of other downloads so that the information could be targeted based on user's context and history data. This is still in development at the time of writing. A typical screen is shown in Figure 2.

4. Mobile system content

The moving server utilised the GPS input as a location device. This was found to be accurate enough for the prototype applications. Only some of these relied on s significant location-awareness. The main *locator* was the fact that the system, was used in proximity to the users, e.g. on a public tram or bus, and the users were essentially a captive audience for a short time. This allowed the download of a large amount of content to the user's devices as and when it was requested. The use of GPS input to the server allowed a level of location-based sponsorship of the content such as advertising banners on the downloaded games related to the local businesses. This was felt to be a better way to target advertising than to rely on ad-hoc Bluetooth adverts or similar systems that have been tried in the past. The advantage being that the user can opt-in to the system and is rewarded for participation.

5. Static system content

The significant difference of the static system to the moving system is the reliance on GPS in the user device to provide rich content. This enabled a few different applications to be developed based on the use of tagged GPS multimedia files. This allowed the user to download the complete content (or a large proportion) at a specified point and then take it in the device until the GPS triggered its use in the relevant context.

The specific applications of this technology are quite wide but the concentration at first was the provision of guided trails and annotated multimedia descriptions of displays in open-air museums.

The use of the system will be further described in the final paper and elaborated on in the conference presentation.

One of the applications still under development is a system situated in the foyer of a theatre enabling context-driven advertising to be delivered based on customer preference by linking to the ticketing system – When tickets are sold the customer receives targeted information for similar events based on buying history – Similar to the buying suggestions offered by online retailers.

6 Analysis of use

The system has been designed and the prototype will be in full operation as part of a wider context-aware location-based information pilot in. At present (April 2008) only the static content (a guided tour) has been developed as this was seen to be a priority system to develop "proof of concept" and to utilise the capability of the chosen platform. Some initial problems occurred with the delay in obtaining GPS signals and the time required to download the material to the user's device causing limits to be imposed for further development in this type of application. It was felt that the initial download would be improved by being supplemented by further download points in the tour path and so a re-design was carried out to incorporate the findings. Whilst it is feasible to download the whole tour at the start it was felt that a better interaction with the user could take place if there were a number of different points of contact. This was seen to enhance the design of the software allowing easier integration of future upgrades such as the contextual interaction mentioned above.

A more detailed analysis of the user's reaction to the system will be available at the conference in September as the project is due to end in summer 2008.

7. Conclusions

Initial reactions to the system have been encouraging. Demonstrations have shown a number of possible applications in action that are being further refined and produced as a more polished set of prototype applications. Interest has been shown from a number of different content providers in numerous different areas from simple advertising to more complex interactive e-learning and health education messaging. The number of different applications has had to be curtailed due to limited funds and time to develop but it is envisaged that the prototype will be further developed in the near future to provide a network of useful information points in both moving public areas and static locations in the region, with a variety of enhancements planned to be added for the interaction between the system and the user.

The use of such an information delivery system that allows users to interact via their own phones assists in the promotion of mobile computing systems as there are fewer issues to learning with the user interface as the phone user should be familiar with a number of the available functions already.

A number of further developments are planned as outlined above: These include an "Informational Treasure hunt" where the tour software is enhanced to include an interactive m-learning component based on local context such as historical monuments or buildings.

Another enhancement is to extend the system to include a sub-system to learn the user's context and so provide more closely targeted information to the user's device rather than using a mass download which could include information already consumed at other points or at other times.

Final conclusions on use, usability and final user reactions will be available at the conference in September.

References

[1] Dennett, C and Traxler J, Project Bluetooth:Support for computing first years, *Proc. HEA ICS 8th Annual conference Southampton, UK August 2007*, available online at http://www.ics.heacademy.ac.uk/events/8th-annual-conf/

[2] Aalto L, Göthlin N, Korhonen J & Ojala T Bluetooth and WAP Push based location-aware mobile advertising system. *Proc. Second International Conference on Mobile Systems, Applications and Services, Boston, MA, 49 - 58*. 2004 Available online at http://www.mediateam.oulu.fi/publications/pdf/496.pdf

[3] Bluetooth Special Interest Group at http://www.bluetooth.com

[4] PyBluez, http://org.csail.mit.edu/pybluez

[5] LightBlue, http://lightblue.sourceforge.net

Comic Layout for Automatic Comic Generation from Game Log

Ruck Thawonmas and Tomonori Shuda

Abstract The paper presents our system for generating comics from game log. In particular, comic layout is focused. In order to achieve more comic-like expressivity, we extend an existing comic layout process proposed by Shamir et al. as follows. First, tiny frames are introduced for being placed vertically in the same row. Second, splash frames taking up space of several rows are introduced for emphasizing the corresponding frames. Third, slant frames are introduced for shooting events. Comic sequences generated with the proposed layout process and with the existing one are compared and discussed.

1 Introduction

Summary of user experiences in an entertaining fashion can help not only augmenting their personal memory but also promoting communication among user communities. Two representative applications are Nokia's Life Blog [1] and Microsoft's MyLifeBits [2]. Both enable individuals to record daily experiences in a form of multimedia contents such as photos and videos.

Our system targets user experiences in games, especially online games. The goal is to summarize player experiences in a game in a form of comics based on their game log. Comic-style representation has been used for summary of conference [3] and diary [4] experiences, as well as video contents [5]. Our work was inspired by a work in [6] that also aims at creating a sequence of comic-like images summarizing

Ruck Thawonmas
Intelligent Computer Entertainment Laboratory, Graduate School of Science and Engineering, Ritsumeikan University, Kusatsu, Shiga, 525-8577, Japan, e-mail: ruck@ci.ritsumei.ac.jp

Tomonori Shuda
Intelligent Computer Entertainment Laboratory, Graduate School of Science and Engineering, Ritsumeikan University, Kusatsu, Shiga, 525-8577, Japan

Please use the following format when citing this chapter:

Thawonmas, R. and Shuda, T., 2008, in IFIP International Federation for Information Processing, Volume 279; *New Frontiers for Entertainment Computing*; Paolo Ciancarini, Ryohei Nakatsu, Matthias Rauterberg, Marco Roccetti; (Boston: Springer), pp. 105–115.

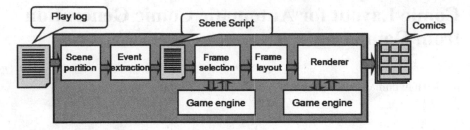

Fig. 1 Overview of the comic generation system.

main game events. The expressivity of comics generated in [6] is, however, limited mainly due to all rows being constrained to the same height.

This paper attempts to achieve more comic-like expressivity by extending the comic layout process in [6]. Our extensions are described in Section 3, after an outline of the comic generation system in Section 2. In Section 4, a comic sequence generated with the proposed layout process from an online game's log is compared to that generated with the layout process in [6] from the same log.

2 Comic Generation System

Figure 1 gives an overview of our system where the input is game log and the output is a resulting comic sequence. Game log consists of a sequence of actions, such as *shoot* and *talk*, recorded when an action is invoked by a player character (PC) or a non-player character (NPC) seen at the user's game client. It is stored at the client side. In order to obtain game events, the game log is processed by the scene partition module and the event extraction module. A game event is a part of play that has interaction level beyond a given threshold. Interaction level at time t, $l(t)$, is defined based on the importance of related actions and that of involving entities (PCs, NPCs, and objects) as

$$l(t) = \sum_a \sum_e \sum_{e'} w_a \max(w_e, w_{e'}) i(t, a, e, e'),$$

where a denote an action; e and e' denote entities; w_a, w_e, and w'_e denote the weights of a, e, and e', respectively, with the range from 0 to 1; and $i(t, a, e, e')$ is 1 if a is performed at t whose subject and object (if any) are e and e', respectively, and 0 otherwise.

The whole play is partitioned into multiple intervals called scenes. This is done at the scene partition module based on $h(t)$ (c.f., Fig. 2.a), a smoothed version of $l(t) - s(t)$, i.e., $h(t) = G(t) * (l(t) - s(t))$, where $G(t)$ is a Gaussian function and $s(t)$ is the number of moves conducted at time t. A scene starts at a point with rising $h(t)$ up from a scene threshold T_s and ends at the starting point of its subsequent scene. Next, for each scene, all intervals with Gaussianly smoothed value of $l(t)$, $G(t) *$

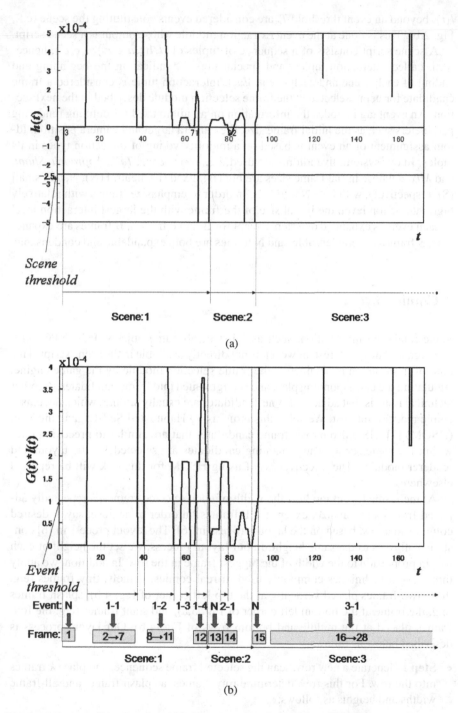

Fig. 2 (a) Scene partition based on $h(t)$, (b) event extraction based on $G(t) * l(t)$.

$l(t)$, beyond an event threshold T_e are considered events constituting the scene (c.f., Fig. 2.b). This is done at the event extraction module whose output is a scene script.

A scene script consists of a sequence of tuples of $(t, l(t, a, e, e'), a, e, e')$, henceforth called interaction tuples, and special tags for indicating the beginning and ending of each scene and each event. Each interaction tuple is considered a frame candidate for being selected at the frame selection module described in the next section. An event tag includes the information on an idiom used for defining rendering parameters such as the initial frame size, the camera target and camera position. Idiom assignment of an event is based on a majority voting of the action types in its tuples. In our system, five idioms are used, i.e., *New Scene*, *Talk*, *Approach*, *Shoot*, and *Mixed* whose initial frame sizes are big (B), fixed (F), neutral (N), N, and small (S), respectively, with $B > N = F > S$. In order to emphasize frames with relatively high interaction level, the initial size of the frame with the largest interaction level in each event is expanded one step, except for B and F frames. B frames are expandable, S frames are condensable, and N frames are both expandable and condensable.

3 Comic Layout

Some rendering information, such as a list of all game objects, PCs, NPCs in a frame candidate of interest, however, is not directly available in the scene script. This kind of information is obtained at the frame selection module by the game engine, simulating the corresponding play, and is augmented into frame candidates. Another technical issue is that adjacent frame candidates are usually similar, which decreases comic readers' interest. We solve this issue using Habituated Self-Organizing Map (HSOM) [7]. HSOM removes frame candidates that are similar to preceding ones within the same scene. The remaining candidates are selected for the layout and renderer modules. The effectiveness of using HSOM for this task will be reported elsewhere.

At the frame layout module, the width of each selected frames is repeatedly adjusted from its initial size, except for F frames, in order to achieve, say, k desired columns in a row, based on the layout process in [6]. The layout process in [6] constrains all rows to the same height. In our layout process, we set the height of each row in proportion to the width of the biggest frame in the row. In addition, we apply three layout techniques commonly used in real comics, namely, tiny frames (e.g. those two frames placed vertically at the top left corner of Fig. 4.b), splash frames (e.g. the frame at the bottom left corner of Fig. 5.a), and slant frames (e.g. the four frames placed at the middle and bottom rows of Fig. 4.b). Our layout process is described below as follows:

- **Step 1** Generate a new row, scan the selected frame sequence, and place k frames into the row. For this row, determine tiny frames, a splash frame, and all frame widths and heights as follows:

- If this row has pairs of S frames, of N and S frames, or of F and S frames, the frames of the first pair will become tiny frames. Place them vertically in the row and consider them as one frame in determination of frame widths described below.
- If this row has a B frame at the beginning, this frame will become a splash frame with the probability P_b. And for the newly defined splash frame, expand its height to cover several rows and associate it to the top row on its right side in determination of frame widths described below.
- Apply the layout process in [6] for determining the widths of all frames in the row. If a splash frame exists, this task will also be done for the remaining rows on its right side. As in [6], if frame widths cannot be determined due to violation of their constraints on allowable widths, set their widths to the same default value, i.e., the width of the N frame.
- Set the row height in proportion to the width of the biggest frame in the row. If a splash frame exists, this task will also be done for the remaining rows on its right side.

- **Step 2** Repeat Step 1 until the sizes of all selected frames are determined.
- **Step 3** Generate slant frames by alternatively upward slanting and downward slanting a row-partition line that satisfies all of the following conditions.

  - it is not the top or bottom page border,
  - there exists at least one *Shoot* frame adjacently above or under it, and
  - there are no *New Scene* frames adjacently under it.

Finally, the resulting comic layout is given to the renderer module for rendering comics. The game engine is used again here to simulate the play at the time of a frame of interest. Such a play is then rendered into an image. In order to achieve comic-like images, the grey-scale filter, median filter and Laplacian filter are applied to the background, characters, and objects in each frame accordingly.

4 Resulting Comic Sequences

We tested our comic generation system with an online game called the ICE[1], under development at the authors' laboratory, where typical online-game missions, such as monster fighting and item trading, are available. A screenshot of the ICE is shown in Fig. 3. The main parameters are $k = 3$, $T_s = -2.5 \times 10^{-4}$, $T_e = 1 \times 10^{-4}$, and $P_b = 0.5$.

Figures 4 and 5 show the first half and second half of a comic sequence generated with the proposed layout process, where frame numbers are superimposed. For comparison, Figs. 6 and 7 show the first half and second half of a comic sequence generated with the existing layout process in [6]. Both comic sequences were from the same game log whose scenes and events were derived in Fig. 2.a and Fig. 2.b,

---

[1] http://www.ice.ci.ritsumei.ac.jp/mmog.html

Fig. 3 The ICE screenshot.

respectively. The corresponding idioms and initial sizes of these 28 frames are as follows: 1: New Scene (B), 2-7: Talk (F), 8-11: Mixed (S), 12: Approach (N), 13: New Scene (B), 14: Approach (N), 15: New Scene (B), 16-19: Shoot (N), 20: Shoot (B), and 21-28: Shoot (N); note that the initial size of frame 20 is B expanded from N because it is the frame with the largest $G(t) * l(t)$ in event 3-1.

The tiny frames in Fig. 4.b, frames 10 and 11, result from the fact that they are two consecutive S frames. The splash frame in Fig. 5.a, frame 20, exists because it is the B frame located at the beginning of the middle row. Slant frames are seen in Figs. 4.b, 5.a, and 5.b because they are related to shooting events.

5 Conclusions and Future Work

This paper described our system for generating comics from game log. To achieve more comic-like expressivity, three extensions to [6] on comic layout were presented. The resulting comic sequence is visually better than a fixed row-height style done in [6]. Our future work includes improvement on camera control, special effects, and story development.

References

1. http://r2.nokia.com/nokia/0,,71739,00.html
2. http://research.microsoft.com/barc/mediapresence/MyLifeBits.aspx
3. Y. Sumi, R. Sakamoto, K. Nakao, and K. Mase, ComicDiary: Representing individual experiences in a comic style, *Ubicomp 2002*, pp. 16–32, 2002.
4. S.B. Cho, K.J. Kim, and K.S. Hwang, Generating Cartoon-Style Summary of Daily Life with Multimedia Mobile Devices, *IEA/AIE 2007*, pp. 135–144, 2007.
5. J. Calic, D.P. Gibson, and N.W. Campbell, Efficient Layout of Comic-like Video Summaries, *IEEE Transactions on Circuits and Systems for Video Technology*, vol. 17(7), pp. 931–936, 2007.
6. A. Shamir, M. Rubinstein, and T. Levinboim, Generating Comics from 3D Interactive Computer Graphics, *IEEE Computer Graphics and Applications*, vol. 26(3), pp. 53–61, 2006.
7. S. Marsland, U. Nehmzow, and J. Shapiro, A real-time novelty detector for a mobile robot, *EUREL European Advanced Robotics Systems Masterclass and Conference*, 2000.

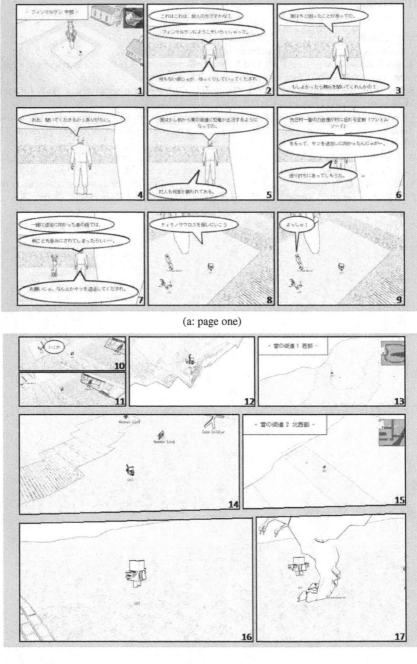

(a: page one)

(b: page two)

Fig. 4 The first half of a comic sequence generated with the proposed layout process: (a) page one and (b) page two.

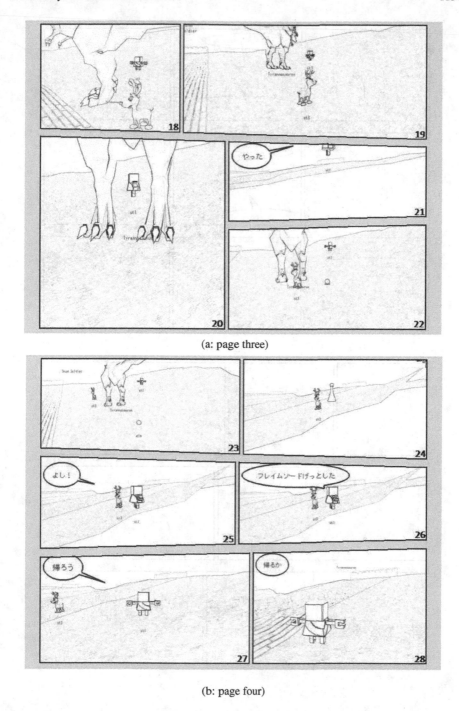

(a: page three)

(b: page four)

Fig. 5 The second half of a comic sequence generated with the proposed layout process: (a) page three and (b) page four.

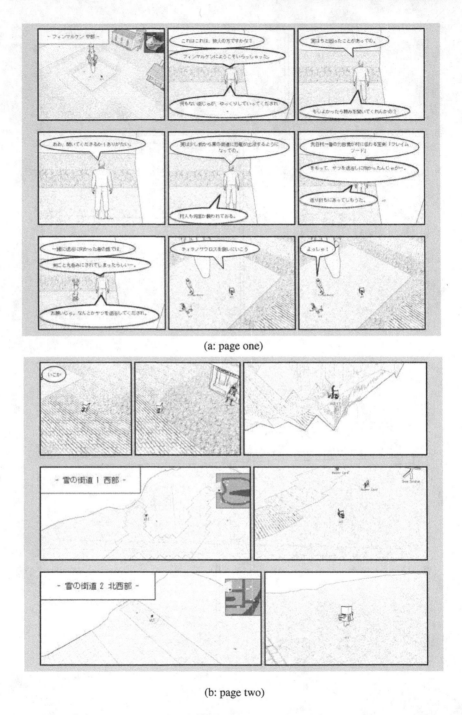

(a: page one)

(b: page two)

Fig. 6 The first half of a comic sequence generated with the existing layout process: (a) page one and (b) page two.

(a: page three)

(b: page four)

Fig. 7 The second half of a comic sequence generated with the existing layout process: (a) page two and (b) page four.

Computing Inspiration: i.plot

Naoko Tosa[1],
Seigow Matsuoka[2], and Ryohei Nakatsu[3]

[1]Kyoto Univeristy, Academic Center for Computing and Media Studies,
Yoshida-Nihon-Matsu, Sakyo, 606-8501 Kyoto, Japan
tosa@media.kyoto-u.ac.jp

[2]Editorial Engineering Laboratory, 7-6-64 Akasaka Minato-ku
107-0052, Tokyo, Japan
[3]National University of Singapore, Interactive Digital Media Institute
4 Engineering Drive 3, Singapore 117576
idmdir@nus.edu.sg

Abstract. In this paper we treat the theme of "the future of narrative." In examining how a computer can inspire with humor and wisdom, we studied the hidden relationships and contextual emergence of language. Pursuing a vision of the future where people will have conversations with robots, we not only display the results visually, but also have a robot agent convey inspiration and emotional content to users.

1 Introduction

Narrative is at its most vivid when emergent technologies are born. "Emergent" means when a product or idea, in the course of its advancement, breaks through a critical barrier, and a heretofore-unimagined paradigm appears. It makes sense that this kind of occurrence can lead to the discovery of new relationships and the creation of fresh images. The trick to finding this kind of emergence is daring to pursue the marriage of completely different ideas.

Since it is expected that the convergence of art and technology will lead society, much thought has been put into the intersection of these two fields. In the history of art and technology, which began in the late 1960's, the one thing that has not been researched enough is the field's relationship to literary narrative. This is perhaps because, due to technological factors, those in the field of literature were not able to approach the interdisciplinary area of art and science. But now, with computers as an inter-medium finally beginning to mature, it has become possible for men and women in the field of literature to get closer to computers.

Please use the following format when citing this chapter:

Tosa, N., Matsuoka, S. and Nakatsu, R., 2008, in IFIP International Federation for Information Processing, Volume 279; *New Frontiers for Entertainment Computing*; Paolo Ciancarini, Ryohei Nakatsu, Matthias Rauterberg, Marco Roccetti; (Boston: Springer), pp. 117–127.

Thus, with "the future of narrative" as a theme, we researched how a computer can offer humor, wisdom and inspiration to a user. Up until now, topics researched within art and science have fallen mainly under the category of nonverbal communication, such as feeling and atmosphere. With our research, the logical meaning of language and its intuitive aspects such as atmosphere and feeling have joined together. We can promise with confidence that in the future, through the addition of narrative technology to art and science, a new, creative "interactive narrativity" will develop, and its developing value will be a significant contribution to the field of art and technology.

2 Inspiration Generation

With traditional context generation and search, words close contextually to a word are chosen by searching through a regular thesaurus. However, with this kind of technique, it is very difficult to produce an interesting context from inspiration will rise out. What is the essence of inspiration? According to the dictionary, it is a new idea that flashes within the creative and speculative process - an idea that did not previously exist in the thinker's mind.

We have realized a method of emergent context generation called Inspiration Computing and developed a system called i.plot. The key feature of i.plot is a system that discovers hidden connections between unrelated words by tracing possible paths through the database. The path between words is like that of a wandering mind, where the jump between each idea is clear but multiple jumps lead to unexpected results. The user may highlight interesting sets of words and delve deeper into the word associations. Other features of i.plot are described below.

3 Technical Realization

The i.plot system is built using open-source software on a Linux platform, and it is accessible via the World Wide Web. The system takes advantage of several publicly available resources and a chaos-based algorithm to produce its inspiration output, using a robot agent to interpret the results.

3.1 Database

With traditional context generation, words close contextually to a word are chosen by searching through a regular thesaurus. However, with this technique, it is difficult to produce interesting results. We have realized a method of emergent context generation we call Inspiration Generation. This method uses a combination of the WordNet lexical database, the Edinburgh Psychological Associative Thesaurus, and Seigow Matsuoka's original "thoughtforms" to produce a dynamic working base with a vocabulary of over 20,000 words.

3.2 Thoughtforms

"Thoughtforms," developed by our collaborator Seigow Matsuoka, are forms for the editing of words. They comprise the following five types:

Concatenation. This is information of the same source group arranged in order of continuity, stratum or ranking, such that the "space" between the separate words matches up. For example, "Top," "middle" and "bottom": they are all words that specify position; they are in a ranked order; and there are no discontinuous jumps between the words.

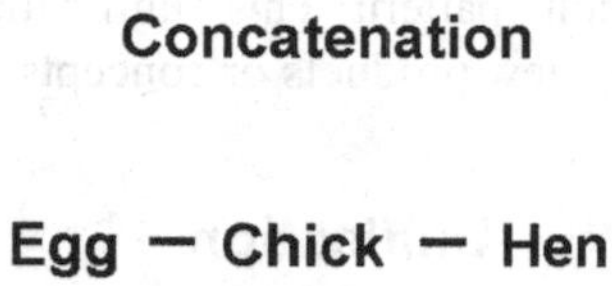

Concatenation

Egg — Chick — Hen

Fig. 1. Concatenation thoughtform example

Balance. Just like "reading, writing and arithmetic" or "food, clothing and shelter," there are many examples of three-sets of words that we use frequently. It is good to find an equally balanced set such that the words push and pull on one another with the same amount of force.

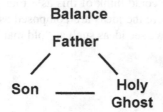

Balance
Father

Son ——— Holy
Ghost

Fig. 2. Balance thoughtform example

Division. This is the division of an idea into two child ideas. Depending on which aspect of the parent we take, the child ideas become separate but complete ideas. So, if we split "computer" into two child ideas, we produce two elements indispensable to a computer.

Division
Hardware
Computer
Software

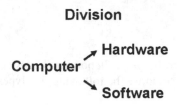

Fig. 3. Division thoughtform example

Unification. A combination of two ideas to produce a new idea. This is not just a simple addition of ideas. This is the creation of a new word or image – a new paradigm – through the combination and synthesis of two ideas. It is also not just a simple reversal of the "division" pattern. This "unification" pattern comes in very handy when trying to develop new products or concepts, or in naming a new idea.

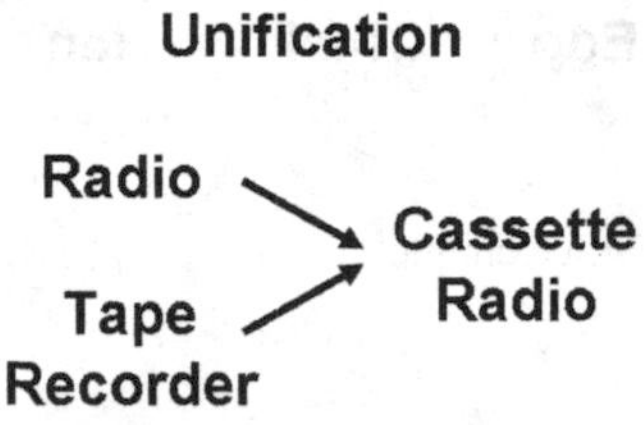

Unification
Radio
Tape Recorder
Cassette Radio

Fig. 4. Unification thoughtform example

Crisscross. This is a pattern in which four ideas are derived from a central idea. There are two types of Crisscross patterns: (1) where the outlying ideas are composed in parallel – one could think of this as a four-point version of the "balance" pattern – and (2) where the ideas are composed as separate axes, creating a grid as below, from which we see ideas such as "old man" and "young woman."

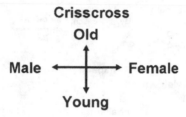

Fig. 5. Crisscross thoughtform example

3.4 Chaos Search

The system uses a dual-synchronized chaos engine, which synchronizes two or more chaos states, to increase the variety of idea-word connections. Each time a user refreshes the display, the entropy of the chaos engine increases. The engine, which runs continuously in the background, contains an Objective chaos, a User chaos following the Objective, and a System value controlling the synchronization of User and Objective. By increasing the System value, the engine produces more chaotic output, and connection lengths vary from short and direct to long and round-about.

3.5 Inspiration Space

This system discovers the hidden connections between words, defining the basic function for each of the other systems.

We collected a database of thoughtform relationships created by students in Japan and added connection data from the Edinburgh Associative Thesaurus (Kiss, et al.), which contains stimulus-response data from a large sample group of people. We define a connection between words to exist if two words are found in the same thoughtform or make up a stimulus-response pair in the associative thesaurus.

The system finds several connections between two unrelated words by tracing a large set of possible paths between the two words, such that the paths traverse several two-word connections. If the chaos engine is in an appropriate state, a preference may be added so that longer paths are displayed, or so that the paths are forced to connection through a more distantly-connected word. The user may further expand the connections of any word of interest.

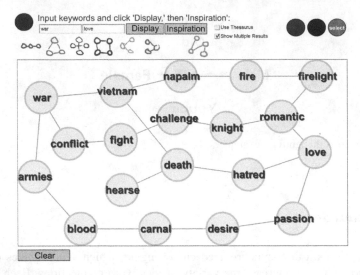

Fig. 6. An example result from Inspiration Space

4 Possible Applications

4.1 *Inspiration Restaurant Guide*

We used information from France Telecom's Yellow Pages database to build a restaurant guide based on our inspiration system.

We entered each of the restaurant categories and locations in Paris into our system, and connected them to related words (i.e. Pizzeria: italian food, tomato; Creperie: date, sweets; Fast Food: quick, cheap). Thus we were able to build inspirational links to each of the restaurant types and physical locations.

The user selects a location (or lets the system choose for him), inputs their preferences for restaurant atmosphere, and a set of words appears. The user can select any word that appears on the screen, and the system searches for a restaurant type closely related to that word. A nearby restaurant of that type is then displayed on the screen.

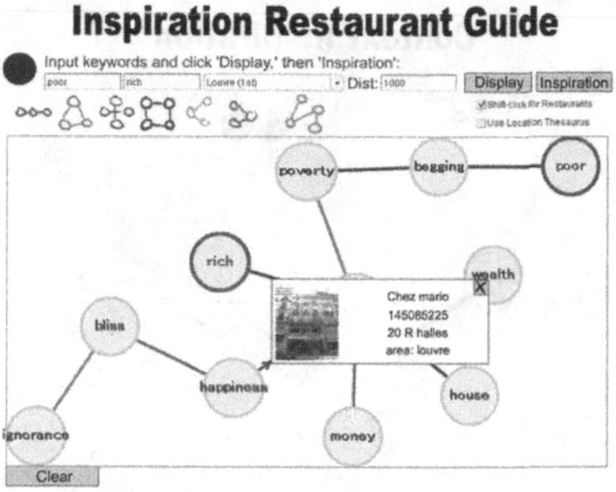

Fig. 7. Example result from Inspiration Restaurant Guide

4.2   Context Inspiration

Using data obtained from the open database WordNet (Princeton University) as well as manual categorization, we classified the words in our database according to their grammatical properties, fitting six categories: who, what, where, when, how, and verb.

The user seeds the system with a few idea words. The system then generates a sentence of various lengths ranging from 2 to 5 words (minus articles, conjunctions, etc.) based on these input words. Wherever there is a blank word, the system fills it in, seeking words inspirationally linked to the words surrounding a blank in the sentence. In the case that there is a word on either side of the blank, we use the same algorithm as for finding a connection between words in the Inspiration Space program, except we look for an intersection point that is of an appropriate grammatical type to fit in the sentence.

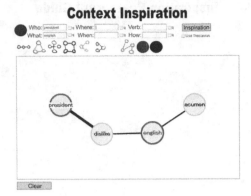

Fig. 8. Example result from Context Inspiration

4.3 Symbol Inspiration

Rather than attaching symbol images onto existing word associations, we created a set of associations directly between symbols. These associations are based on the thoughtforms explained above, where connections are based on geometric forms.

One can either seed the engine by entering in words linked to images in the input textboxes, or by clicking one of the colored thoughtform buttons at the top of the screen. One can select various images to expand the relationships.

By inserting an element of unpredictability from the chaos engine, the connections between images may shift and change, avoiding the draw of logic.

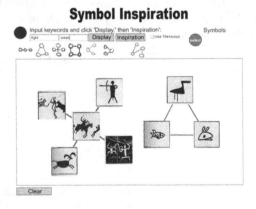

Fig. 9. Example result from Symbol Inspiration

4.4 Inspiration Blog

The blog system adds the ability to take complete sentences as input. Connections between key words in the sentence are all considered, and intersecting words are displayed on the screen. The connections between each entry and the preceding entry are also included, so that the context generated within each entry is continuous.

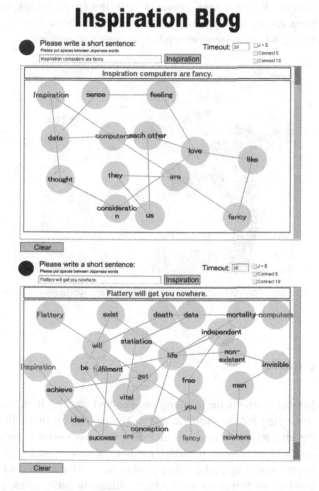

Fig. 10. Example result from Inspiration Blog

5 Robot Agent

Pursuing a vision of the future where people will have conversations with robots, we not only display the results visually, but also have a robot agent convey inspiration and emotional content to users. The robot takes the output and delivers it with behaviors, tai-chi motions and emotional voice synthesis appropriate to the inspiration words. We connected a text-to-speech synthesis engine with the robot, enabling it to perform emotional behaviors and graceful motions in communication with humans. When a user interacts with the inspiration system, the key words are extracted by the system and converted into behaviors via a language-emotion mapping, which the system sends to the robot to perform.

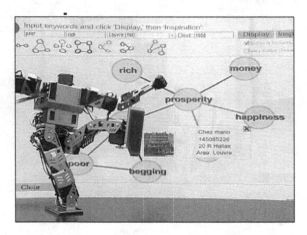

Fig. 11. The robot agent presenting a result from Inspiration Restaurant Guide

6 Future work

Among traditional methods for teaching an idea and passing it on, there exists the method of conveying information via story. The next thing that will become necessary for the interaction technology and expression between computers and humans is research in interactive narrative methods. Our research will likely have a significant impact in this up-and-coming field of interactive narrative methods.

Among the human computer interaction within our daily lives, there are still many logical, simple and boring interactions. Our research, in providing users with inspiration containing humor and wisdom, offers people new opportunities for stimulation; our future symbiosis with computers as well as digital contents (education, games and entertainment) will therefore change significantly, in that computers and robots will convey to people the relationships, breadth of meaning and context hidden between words not easily struck upon by people.

References

1. Janet H. Murray, "Hamlet on the Holodeck".
2. Bela Balazs, "Film theory".
2. Joe Bates, et al. "Oz Project".
3. WordNet (Princeton University, http://www.cogsci.princeton.edu/~wn/)
4. Edinburgh Associative Thesaurus (Kiss, et al.; http://www.eat.rl.ac.uk/)

Analysis and Generation of Japanese Folktales Based on Vladimir Propp's Methodology

Takenori Wama[1], Ryohei Nakatsu[2]

1 Kwansei Gakuin University, School of Science and Technology
2-1 Gakuen, Sanda, 669-1337 Japan
scbc0057@ksc.kwansei.ac.jp
http://www.ksc.kwansei.ac.jp
2 National University of Singapore, Interactive & Digital Media Institute
Block E3A, #02-04, 7 Engineering Drive 1, Singapore 117574
idmdir@nus.edu.sg
http://www.idmi.nus.edu.sg

Abstract. We aim to develop an automatic generation of interactive stories. For this aim, we have analyzed Japanese folktales. In this area, there exists famous research conducted by Vladimir Propp. He analyzed more than 100 Russian magic-inspired folktales by segmenting each of them into a series of short segments and classified each segment into one of 31 functions. Here, we tried to analyze about 20 Japanese folktales adopting his method and found several interesting facts that differentiate Japanese folktales from those of Russia.

Keywords: Storytelling, Interactive Story, Folktales, Functions

1 Introduction

When we want to accomplish something, we always have some kind of story in mind. Furthermore, when we look back at our past, it appears as a series of events. This is the reason why it is sometimes said that "life is just like a story."

After all, story is an essential element in our lives. The existence itself of words such as "*parody*" and "*homage,*" which imply artworks inspired by original works, means that the stories contained in various kinds of artworks have attracted many people.

Vladimir Propp [1] is the leading expert in the field of storytelling. He hypothesized that a story consists of a concatenation of short plots called "*functions*." Based on this idea, he analyzed more than 100 Russian magic-inspired folktales and found that about 30 functions are enough to construct all of the folk-

Please use the following format when citing this chapter:

Wama, T. and Nakatsu, R., 2008, in IFIP International Federation for Information Processing, Volume 279; *New Frontiers for Entertainment Computing*; Paolo Ciancarini, Ryohei Nakatsu, Matthias Rauterberg, Marco Roccetti; (Boston: Springer), pp. 129–137.

tales. Of course, there were lots of predecessors. For example, the Brothers Grimm, known for "*the Grimm Fairy Tales*," collected various kinds of folktales, and such folktale collections helped in analyses of folktales. Although there were other classifications by Wundt and others at that time, Propp thought those classifications were not sufficient, especially in the case of Russian magic folktales. He succeeded in extracting the essence of "story" based on his concept of "*function*."

The approach described in this paper is based on Propp's idea. Our target is to develop an "Interactive Folktale System" taking Japanese folktales as an example, and for this purpose we analyzed Japanese folktales. If it were possible to classify not only magic folktales but also folktales in general, particularly Japanese ones in this work, according to his methodology, we could develop a database of "short stories" by segmenting Japanese folktales and try to develop a support system of story generation using the database.

As a famous tool for story generation, "*Dramatica*" [2] (Screen Play System, Inc.) has been developed for the US movie industry. It enables producers to drastically cut the cost of moviemaking, which is generally very expensive, and has attracted much attention. It asks users various questions concerning stories, and based on their answers gives them materials and advice for story generation. In Japan, too, the study of story generation has become active in recent years [3].

If we succeeded in constructing such automatic story generation systems or story-generation support systems, it would be very easy for any user, not only movie directors and screenplay writers, to generate stories at any time. This would result in greater diversity of contents and surely extend the range of "Entertainment" [4]. If we applied such a system in the field of education, it would help the process of juvenile cultivation of aesthetic sentiments. The following sections of this paper describe Propp's methodology and our analysis of Japanese folktales utilizing it.

2   Theory and Background

Vladimir Propp analyzed more that 100 magic-inspired Russian folktales based on the hypothesis that a story consists of a concatenation of short plots [1]. He tried to classify the short plots extracted from those magic folktales and found that there are 31 categories and that these are sufficient to construct all of the Russian magic folktales. However, as he himself pointed out, his methodology works well specifically for Russian magic folktales, which form a particular category among folktales in general.

2.1 Thirty-one Functions of Propp

Propp arrived at an interesting conclusion through the process of analyzing Russian magic folktales. He found that different characters in the field of folktales achieve similar actions frequently. These acts are regularly used as universal material and fundamental components of folktales, and he called them *"functions."* Table 1 shows the 31 functions of Propp.

Based on his finding that the number of functions is restricted, he conjectured that the ordinal succession of functions in each magic folktale is always constant. Figure 1 shows the basic structure of the folktales found and proposed by him.

Table 1. Thirty-one functions

[Code]Function	
0. [α] Initial situation	16. [H] The hero struggles with the villain
1. [β] Absentation	17. [J] Branding or marking the hero
2. [γ] Interdiction	18. [I] Victory over the villain
3. [δ] Violation	19. [K] The liquidation of misfortune or lack
4. [ε] Reconnaissance	
5. [ζ] Delivery	20. [$\downarrow$] Return of the hero
6. [η] Trickery	21. [Pr] Pursuit of the hero
7. [θ] Complicity	22. [Rs] Rescue of the hero
8. [A] Villainy	23. [O] Unrecognized arrival
9. [B] Mediation, the connective incident	24. [L] Claims of a false hero
10. [C] Consent to counteraction	25. [M] Difficult task
11. [$\uparrow$] Departure, dispatch of the hero from home	26. [N] Solution of a task
	27. [Q] Recognition of the hero
12. [D] The first function of the donor	28. [Ex] Exposure of the false hero
13. [E] Reaction of the hero	29. [T] Transfiguration
14. [F] The acquisition, receipt of a marginal agent	30. [U] Punishment of the false hero or villain
15. [G] Transference to a designated place; guidance	31. [W] Wedding

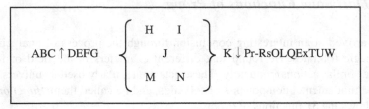

Fig. 1. Basic structure

2.2 Signification and Potentiality

As mentioned at the beginning of this chapter, Propp himself pointed out that the above rule holds true for Russian magic folktales but is not generally applicable to narratives, especially artificially produced tales. Propp's idea, in other words, represents only the characteristics of the Russian magic folktales he analyzed. Although some researchers tried to apply it to constructing a support system for story generation, in most cases the materials they study involve Russian magic folktales, similar to the work of Propp [5] [6]. Taking these situations into consideration, any attempt to apply his methodology to Japanese folktales would seem contradictory. However, if it could be shown that his methodology is applicable to Japanese folktales, this would imply that his idea could be applied to various fields, thus facilitating the construction of a system that can automatically generate various types of stories.

3 Analysis of Story

Japanese folktales are alive and well in diverse ways [7]. Folktales are essentially handed down orally from parent to child or from grandparent to grandchild. The descriptions used in relaying the story, as a matter of course, depend mainly on specific speakers who try to entertain their audience by telling these stories. This causes some differences even in the same folktale from one locality to another, or even from one family to another. We picked out more than 20 Japanese folktales from a popular folktale book [8] published in Japan for the purpose of maintaining consistency. In the following sections, analyses are given for "*Momotaro*" and "*Click-Clack Mountain*" as two examples of Japanese folktales.

3.1 *"Momotaro" (The Adventures of a Peach boy)*

As is common in most folktales, the prologue of the story begins with the "Initial situation" [α] (ex. long, long time ago in a certain place...). The circumstances and scene including the main characters become clear, and then the story revolves around these characters.

Table 2 shows an analysis of *"Momotaro."* It begins with the "Initial situation" and revolves around Momotaro, a leading character. He grows up fast and comes to have a determination to get rid of the devils that are endangering the villagers. On the way to Demon's Island, he meets a dog, a monkey, and a pheasant, and he makes them his companions by giving them "Kibidango," a sweet millet dumpling. Up hill, down dale, and across the sea, his group finally arrives at their destination, Demon's Island. They punish devils to get back stolen property. Finally, they make a triumphant return to Momotaro's village. Figure 2 shows the structure of *"Momotaro"* based on the model of Figure 1.

Table 2. Analysis of *"Momotaro"*

Text	Function
Long, long time ago in a certain place, there were some grandparents. *snip*	[α] Initial situation
One day, when the grandmother was at the riverside doing laundry, she saw a big peach floating down from upriver. *snip*	[Q] Recognition of the hero
Up hill and down dale, Momotaro and his group got to the seashore. *snip*	[G] Transference to a designated place
"I'm Momotaro, the strongest in Japan, punishing you devils!" *snip*	[H] The hero struggles with the villain
They made it back to his Grandparents safely.	[↓] Return of the hero

$$\alpha \ \text{QBC} \uparrow \text{DEFDEFDEFGHI} \downarrow$$

Fig. 2. Structure of "*Momotaro*"

3.2 "Click-Clack Mountain" (Return of a Rabbit)

Table 3 shows an analysis of "*Click-Clack Mountain.*" It also begins with the "Initial situation," and the main characters, again Grandparents, are explained in turn. Although the grandfather punishes a mischievous raccoon, the grandmother is killed by this shifty animal while the grandfather is away. He is disconsolate at her death, and then a rabbit, a friend of the Grandparents, inspires the determination to seek revenge against the raccoon for the murder. The rabbit burns the raccoon at the stake using flint, hitting the notes "*Click-Clack,*" the onomatopoeia behind this folktale, and rubs pepper, disguised as medicine, into the raccoon's wounds. Finally, the rabbit puts the raccoon in a ship of mud and sinks it with the raccoon to the bottom of the river. Figure 3 shows the structure of "*Click-Clack Mountain*" based on the model of Figure 1.

Table 3. Analysis of "*Click-Clack Mountain*"

Text	Function
Long, long ago in a certain place, there were some good-hearted Grandparents.	[α] Initial situation
snip	
Grandfather caught Raccoon swathed in a rope.	[U] Punishment of a false hero or villain
snip	
Shifty Raccoon had an evil design to get out of here.	[η] Trickery
snip	
Rabbit living in the front mountain, seeing Grandfather disconsolate at her death, consoled him and gave him the determination to avenge himself on Raccoon.	[C] Consent to counter-action
snip	

Raccoon saw the firewood in his back burst into flames. *snip*	[A] Villainy

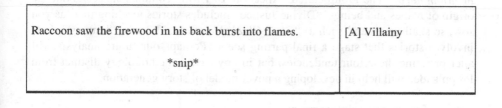

Fig. 3. Structure of "*Click-Clack Mountain*"

4 Discussion

"*Function*" as defined by Propp represents just the action of the characters. In other words, function itself contains a role of subject or object in a short scene. For example, with the eleventh function in Table 1, [↑] Departure, the composition of "the hero leaves his home" is predetermined. Also for the eighteenth function, [I] Victory over the villain, the condition that "A works on B" is included in the function. In this case, A is a hero and B is a villain (a hero defeated a villain) or A is a villain and B is a hero (villain is defeated by a hero). From these examples, it seems the reason why the roles of main characters are included in the definition of each function is that the main characters have some kind of symbolism. Devils in "*Momotaro*" and Raccoon in "*Click-Clack Mountain*" are emblematic of an adversary that threatens the lives and livelihoods of people. Furthermore, we can assume that Propp realized the symbolism in the magic folktales he analyzed, so he may have hypothesized the concatenation of short plots called "*functions*" as having a role system of subject-object relationships. Through our analysis, we found that this is true in the case of Japanese folktales.

We noted an interesting factor while analyzing more than 20 Japanese folktales based on Propp's methodology. Rabbit in "*Click-Clack Mountain*" plays second fiddle in the early part, which features Grandparents and Raccoon; however, Rabbit stands in the spotlight, as if a leading character, in the later part of the story. On the other hand, "*Momotaro*" has a clearly established role of hero, and the behavior of each character changes little in this story. This seems to suggest that a certain regularity may be found by analyzing Japanese folktales in more detail.

A new classification of Japanese folktales taking a different approach from Propp's idea is also under review. Table 4 shows four provisional groups of Japanese folktales. We hypothesized that folktales classified as "Grand Finale" bring the story to an end by punishing villains, or otherwise resolving a problem, as seen in "*Momotaro*." The group called "Anecdote of Birth" contains stories about the origin of names and beings. "Divine Justice" includes stories teaching that 'as you sow, so shall you reap,' such as "*Click-Clack Mountain*." Finally, "Estrangement" involves stories that stage a final parting scene. Perhaps our future analysis will alter or refine these four tendencies, but in any case a methodology distinct from Propp's idea will help in developing a novel model of story generation.

Table 4. Four provisional story groups

1.	Grand Finale
2.	Anecdote of Birth
3.	Divine Justice
4.	Estrangement

5   Conclusions

This paper describes the approach of applying Propp's methodology to a category of Japanese folktales. We anticipated many hurdles because we tried to analyze Japanese folktales rather than the Russian ones he analyzed. However, we could successfully analyze 20 representative Japanese folktales by utilizing the 31 functions defined by Propp. At the same time, we found that there is no single basic storyline, as in the case of Russian folktales, but several basic storylines. By carefully analyzing each story, we found that there are basically four representative storylines in the case of Japanese folktales: grand finale, anecdote of origin, divine justice, and estrangement. We also found interesting phenomena such as the role of character behavior, i.e., whether there are any transitions in a character's behavior, and a methodology distinct from Propp's was explored. Based on our findings, we are now trying to develop a model of generating Japanese folktales. This will require, in keeping with this approach, an increase in the number of analyzed folktales beyond 20, from the viewpoint of developing a model. In addition, we should not only make a database of "stories" according to their "*function*" segmentations but also develop a support system for story generation using our own way of concatenating short plots. As the concept of "storytelling" [9] has recently attracted much attention, we can expect that related fields will become even hotter pursuits in the future.

References

1. Propp, V. (1968). *Morphology of the Folktale*. University of Texas Press.

2. Tutani, Y. YUZI's INDIE FILMMAKER. (2003).
   http://www.voltage.co.jp/indiefm/dramatica/dramatica1.htm.
3. Kaneko, M. Scenario Engine Project. (2003).
   http://www.teu.ac.jp/clab/orc/pdf/scenario2003.pdf.
4. Nakatsu, R. & Rauterberg, M. *A New Framework for Entertainment Computing: From Passive to Active Experience.* (2005). In: F. Kishino et al. (Eds.), *Entertainment Computing ICEC'05* (pp.1-12). *Lecture Notes in Computer Science*, Vol.3711, Springer Press..
5. Sakuma, T. & Ogata, T. Story Generation Support System used the Story Theory of Propp. (2005). *The 19th Annual Conference of the Japanese Society for Artificial Intelligence*, 3D3-04.
6. Sakuma, T. & Ogata, T. The Synthesis of Stories using Combine Rules: An Approach for the Story Generation Support System with Automatic Story Generation Function. (2006). *The 20th Annual Conference of the Japanese Society for Artificial Intelligence*, 2E3-2.
7. Inada, K. *Japanese Folktales Hand Book.* (2001). Sanseido Publisher.
8. Tomomi, K. *Classical Edition: Japanese Folktales 101.* (1997). Kodansha.
9. Murray, J. H. *Hamlet on the Holodeck: The Future of Narrative in Cyberspace.* (1997). Free Press.